MASTERING BASIC SKILLS
THIRD GRADE

Brighter Child®
An imprint of Carson-Dellosa Publishing LLC
Greensboro, North Carolina

An imprint of Carson-Dellosa Publishing, LLC
P.O. Box 35665
Greensboro, NC 27425-5665

carsondellosa.com

Printed in the USA. All rights reserved.
ISBN 978-1-4838-0108-7

01-002141151

Table of Contents

Table of Contents

Contents by Skill

Contents by Skill

Introduction

Welcome to *Mastering Basic Skills*. In third grade, children are introduced to many new and difficult skills. Third graders use comprehension skills with their reading; they are able to write a paragraph with a main idea and supporting details; they know how to use a dictionary; and they can identify the plot, setting, and main characters of a story. Third graders' math skills have also increased to include multiplication, division, and more sophisticated problem solving. Many third graders will have nightly homework and will begin to write and present simple reports.

Third grade is an academic year where children make great emotional and academic leaps. The essential skills that are being taught are more difficult. They are now reading chapter books and applying math to real-world situations. Writing is no longer done simply for practice but now has a purpose. Eager eight- and nine-year-olds are ready for these new challenges, but many have developed an "I-know-it-all" attitude and claim they are ready to take on anything that is handed their way.

Although many third graders may seem fairly confident, they still need much praise, guidance, support, and encouragement. Because they are so eager to learn (and enjoy showing off their knowledge), they sometimes will take on more than they are actually ready to handle. Children need guidance so they do not become frustrated or too self-critical when things get difficult.

Third grade children like the idea of setting goals and are able to work independently for longer periods of time. They have an understanding of choices and realize that there are consequences for making wrong choices. They are learning how to work together cooperatively and how to provide some give-and-take—these are the beginnings of the ability to compromise.

The puzzles, games, drills, and activities provided in this book will challenge children while providing them with meaningful practice. They will be able to show off their skills and have fun at the same time. That is a great combination!

Everyday Ways to Enrich Learning Experiences

Language Arts

The single most important skill that a child needs for success in school, and later in life, is to be literate. In other words, children must learn how to read. You can do many things to encourage literacy.

- Encourage your child to read every day. Begin introducing chapter books. Have your child read a chapter a day.
- Children at this age still love to be read to. Take turns reading together. When your child comes to an unknown word, help your child determine the meaning of the word, using either context clues or a dictionary.
- Ask questions. Have your child guess what is going to happen next or make up a new ending for a story.
- Read fables, folktales, and myths from diverse cultures together. Ask your child to explain the moral or lesson of the story.
- Go to the library and let your child choose new books.
- Ask your child to compare and contrast two of his or her favorite books.
- Write stories together. Have your child illustrate the stories.
- Have your child keep a writing notebook where he or she can write stories, opinion pieces, or narratives about things he or she has done.
- Have your child make a comic book.
- Fill your child's environment with literacy materials like magnetic letters, books, magazines, newspapers, catalogs, paper, pencils, crayons, paints, and CDs.
- Encourage your child to write thank-you notes or letters.
- Together, make a scrapbook of third grade memories.
- Supervise your child's use of the Internet. Search for stories, games, and learning activities that your child can enjoy online.
- Have your child pick a topic that interests him or her. Then, help your child find information about the topic on the Internet. Encourage your child to write about what he or she has learned.
- Take your child to a play or some type of theatrical production.
- Encourage your child to read and write poetry.
- Ask your child to look through the newspaper for information: weather, sports, local events, national news, comics, and movie listings.

Math and Science

Many toys and puzzles provide young children with early math and science learning experiences. Remember to point out all the ways we use numbers and science in our daily lives. Here are some suggested activities.

- Provide blocks, puzzles, and other building materials for your child to manipulate.
- Make a collage of quadrilaterals cut out from colorful construction paper. Have your child identify any shared attributes between quadrilaterals. For instance, rhombuses and rectangles both have four sides.
- Encourage play with magnets, scales, and science books and kits.
- Have your child practice using mental math with addition, subtraction, multiplication, and division.
- Make up word problems with your child while cooking dinner, at the grocery store, or driving around town.
- Look for numbers in magazines, books, billboards, or menus. Have your child round any whole numbers he or she sees to the nearest 10 or 100.
- Use snack time to help your child learn more about equivalent fractions. Cut an apple into $\frac{1}{2}$ and cut another apple into $\frac{1}{4}$ to show that they are equal.
- Help your child learn basic math facts. Play basic fact games.
- Have your child help you in the kitchen. Give your child liquids to measure or objects to weigh using standard units.
- Give your child boxes to measure and, for an extra challenge, ask your child to calculate the perimeter and area of the box.
- Play card games. This can help children learn to add quickly.
- Visit science and children's museums.
- Talk about how we use numbers in the real world: telling time, buying groceries, paying bills, and so on.
- Give your child a watch and encourage him or her to tell time to the nearest minute.
- Go on a nature walk with your child. Help him or her gather data during the walk then make a bar graph or line plot representing the data. For instance, create a graph that shows how many different insects your child found on a walk.
- Encourage your child to begin a hobby. Encourage individual interests.
- Encourage an interest in music.

Recommended Books for Third Graders

A

The Adventures of Ali Baba Bernstein by
Johanna Hurwitz
Alexander, Who Used to Be Rich Last
Sunday by Judith Viorst
The Amazing Bone by William Steig
Andrew Wants a Dog by Steven Kroll
Animal Cafe by John Stadler

B

The Book of Pigericks: Pig Limericks
by Arnold Lobel
Brother Eagle, Sister Sky: A Message from
Chief Seattle, paintings by Susan Jeffers

C

Cam Jansen and the Mystery of the
Dinosaur Bones by David A. Adler
Cam Jansen and the Mystery of the
Television Dog by David A. Adler
Camp Ghost-Away by Judy Delton
Charlotte's Web by E. B. White
The Chinese Siamese Cat by Amy Tan
The Courage of Sarah Noble
by Alice Dalgliesh

D

Digging Up Dinosaurs by Aliki
Dinosaur Hunters by Kate McMullan

E

The Emperor's New Clothes by Hans
Christian Andersen

F

Fin M'Coul: The Giant of Knockmany Hill,
retold and illustrated by Tomie de Paola
Flat Stanley by Jeff Brown
Flatfoot Fox and the Case of the Missing
Whoooo by Eth Clifford
Freckle Juice by Judy Blume
Funnybones by Janet and Allan Ahlberg

G

George Washington's Breakfast
by Jean Fritz
Girl from the Snow Country by Masako
Hidaka
Grandfather Four Winds and Rising Moon
by Michael Chanin
Grasshopper on the Road by Arnold Lobel

H

Harry and the Terrible Whatzit
by Dick Gackenbach
Harry Potter books by J. K. Rowling
Helen Keller: Toward the Light by Stewart
Graff and Polly Anne Graff
Homer Price by Robert McCloskey

I

Imogene's Antlers by David Small
In Trouble with Teacher by Patricia Brennan
Demuth

J

Jackie Robinson and the Story of All-Black
Baseball by Jim O'Connor
Just a Dream by Chris Van Allsburg
Just Plain Fancy by Patricia Polacco

K

Knots on a Counting Rope by Bill Martin, Jr.
and John Archambault

L

The Legend of the Indian Paintbrush, retold
and illustrated by Tomie de Paola
The Legend of the Bluebonnet: An Old Tale
of Texas, retold and illustrated by Tomie
de Paola
A Light in the Attic by Shel Silverstein
The Lorax by Dr. Seuss
Lyle, Lyle, Crocodile by Bernard Waber

M

Mag the Magnificent by Dick Gackenbach
Magic School Bus books by Joanna Cole
Making a New Home in America by
    Maxine B. Rosenberg
Maurice's Room by Paula Fox
Matreshka by Becky Hickox Ayres
The Miss Nelson books by Harry Allard and
    James Marshall
The Missing Piece Meets the Big O by Shel
    Silverstein
Miss Rumphius by Barbara Cooney
*The Monster in the Third Dresser Drawer
    and Other Stories about Adam Joshua*
    by Janice Lee Smith
Mousekin's Golden House by Edna Miller
Muggie Maggie by Beverly Cleary
*My Painted House, My Friendly Chicken,
    and Me* by Maya Angelou

N

Nate the Great books by Marjorie
    Weinman Sharmat
The New Kid on the Block: Poems
    by Jack Prelutsky
Nice New Neighbors by Franz Brandenberg
No Coins, Please by Gordon Korman
Nothing Ever Happens on My Block
    by Ellen Raskin

P

The Patchwork Quilt by Valerie Flournoy
Paul Bunyan: A Tall Tale, retold and
    illustrated by Steven Kellogg
Paul Revere by Jan Gleiter and Kathleen
    Thompson
Perfect, the Pig by Susan Jeschke
Pippi Goes on Board by Astrid Lindgren
The Polar Express by Chris Van Allsburg

R

Ramona Quimby, Age 8 by Beverly Cleary
Random House Book of Poetry for Children,
    selected and introduced by Jack
    Prelutsky
Rats on the Roof and Other Stories by
    James Marshall
The Relatives Came by Cynthia Rylant

S

*Sebastian (Super Sleuth) and the Copycat
    Crime* by Mary Blount Christian
The Spooky Tail of Prewitt Peacock
    by Bill Peet
Stone Fox by John Reynolds Gardiner
Sylvester and the Magic Pebble
    by William Steig

T

Thank You, Amelia Bedelia by Peggy Parish
Treasure Nap by Juanita Havill
*Tyrannosaurus Was a Beast: Dinosaur
    Poems* by Jack Prelutsky

U

Uncle Vova's Tree by Patricia Polacco

W

The Wild Christmas Reindeer by Jan Brett
The Wizard of Oz by L. Frank Baum
The Wump World by Bill Peet

Y

Yoo Hoo, Moon! by Mary Blocksma

Third Grade Skills Checklist

This list is an overview of some of the key skills learned in third grade. When using this list, please keep in mind that the curriculum will vary across the United States, as will how much an individual teacher is able to teach over the course of one year. The list will give you an overview of the majority of third grade skills and assist you in motivating, guiding, and helping your child maintain or even increase skills.

Language Arts/Reading

Recognizes beginning blends: bl, cl, fl, gl, pl, sl, br, cr, dr, fr, gr, pr, tr, sk, sm, sn, sp, st, sw, tw, scr, spl, spr, str..❏

Recognizes digraphs: ai, ay, ee, ea, oa, ue, ui, oo.....................................❏

Recognizes r-controlled vowels: ir, ur, er, ar, or ....❏

Recognizes diphthongs: au, aw, ew, oi, ou, ow, oy...................................❏

Recognizes beginning digraphs: ch, sh, th, ph, qu ....❏

Recognizes ending blends: -mp, -nd, -nk, -lk, -sk, -nt, -ft, -st...................❏

Recognizes ending digraphs: -ch, -sh, -th, -ng, -dge ....❏

Recognizes silent letters in consonant combinations: kn, wr, -ck, -mb, -tch ....❏

Recognizes compound words..❏

Recognizes contractions..❏

Recognizes antonyms, synonyms, and homonyms ....❏

Discriminates between nouns, verbs, adjectives, adverbs, and prepositions.............❏

Recognizes subject and predicate ....❏

Uses plurals: -s and -es ....❏

Can divide words into syllables ....❏

Can identify the main idea of a story ....❏

Can identify the conclusion of a story ....❏

Can identify cause and effect relationships in a story ....❏

Can make predictions from context clues...❏

Draws illustrations to match sentences ....❏

Uses correct punctuation: period, question mark, exclamation point ....❏

Identifies types of sentences ....❏

Can use a dictionary, thesaurus, and encyclopedia ....❏

Can identify prefixes and suffixes...❏

Can write a descriptive paragraph..❏

Can write a persuasive paragraph ....❏

Is able to construct a short story ....❏

Is beginning to read and write for pleasure ....❏

Math

Recognizes odd and even numbers .... ❏

Reads and writes numbers 0 to 9,999 .... ❏

Understands place value to the ten thousands place .... ❏

Knows relation and comparison symbols <, > and = ... ❏

Can complete simple patterns .... ❏

Performs two-digit addition, with regrouping .... ❏

Performs two-digit subtraction, with regrouping .... ❏

Performs three-digit addition, with regrouping .... ❏

Performs three-digit subtraction, with regrouping .... ❏

Knows multiplication facts to 9 .... ❏

Knows division facts to 9 .... ❏

Can multiply one-digit numbers by two-digit numbers .... ❏

Can multiply two-digit numbers by three-digit numbers .... ❏

Can divide one-digit numbers into two-digit numbers without remainders ..... ❏

Can divide one-digit numbers into two-digit numbers with remainders .... ❏

Is able to solve story problems using multiplication and division .... ❏

Can sequence events .... ❏

Understands symmetry .... ❏

Can write number sentences using +, –, and = ... ❏

Can read, interpret, and create a bar graph and line graph .... ❏

Can count money using coins in combination to $10.00 .... ❏

Can tell time in five-minute intervals .... ❏

Can estimate elasped time to the hour .... ❏

Understands the concept of area and perimeter .... ❏

Can measure items using standard units .... ❏

Can identify fractions to $\frac{1}{10}$ (unit and denominator) .... ❏

Can add and subtract fractions with common denominators .... ❏

Uses problem-solving strategies to complete math problems .... ❏

Cursive Letter Practice

Trace and write the uppercase and lowercase cursive letters.

Aa   Bb   Cc

Dd   Ee   Ff

Gg   Hh   Ii

Jj   Kk   Ll

Mm   Nn

Oo   Pp   Qq

Rr   Ss   Tt

Uu   Vv   Ww

Xx   Yy   Zz

Cursive Writing Evaluation

Copy the poem in your best cursive handwriting.

There was a rabbit

With a bad habit

Of jumping on places

Like crocodiles' faces!

Short and Long Vowels Review

Read each sentence. Listen to the first vowel in the highlighted word.
Write ˘ or – over the vowel and circle the correct word after the sentence.

1. Ray skied down the **slope**.   long   short
2. I put my picture inside a **frame**.   long   short
3. The **kite** was flying high in the air.   long   short
4. I asked Sean to **toss** the ball to me.   long   short
5. Ann picked a **bunch** of flowers from the field.   long   short
6. Tina is Marie's **sister**.   long   short
7. Put those papers in the **trash**.   long   short
8. I sat on the **bench** in the park.   long   short
9. The **tube** of toothpaste was empty.   long   short
10. Put **those** books on the shelf.   long   short
11. I need to get out of the sun and sit in the **shade**.   long   short
12. Lisa wore a white **dress** to the party.   long   short

Number Patterns

Study each sequence of numbers.
Circle the group of numbers that continues the pattern.

A. 1, 3, 5, 7, 9, . . .

        10, 11, 12, 13   11, 13, 15, 17   12, 14, 16, 18

B. 3, 6, 9, 12, 15, . . .

        18, 21, 24, 27   16, 17, 18, 19   30, 60, 90, 120

C. 1, 4, 7, 10, . . .

        12, 14, 16, 18   11, 12, 13, 14   13, 16, 19, 22

D. 1, 7, 13, 19, . . .

        21, 28, 34, 40   25, 31, 37, 43   21, 23, 25, 27

Ordering Numbers

Rewrite the numbers in each row in order from **least** to **greatest**.

A. 6,283   683   561   656   _____ _____ _____ _____

B. 8,899   882   8,311   411   _____ _____ _____ _____

Rewrite the numbers in each row in order from **greatest** to **least**.

C. 737   3,778   7,138   397   _____ _____ _____ _____

D. 998   899   9,989   9,998   _____ _____ _____ _____

Long and Short Vowels Assessment

For each word, write ⌣ or – over the vowel that correctly completes the word. Write the letter on the line.

1. wr___ck	e u	5. tr___sh	a e	9. r___le	u a
2. spr___ng	u e	6. ch___me	e i	10. bl___ze	e a
3. h___me	e o	7. sc___pe	i o	11. c___mmon	o u
4. f___lm	a i	8. s___ze	a i	12. t___be	u a

BONUS

Divide a sheet of paper into two columns. Write the long vowel words from above in one column and the short vowel words in the other column.

Addition Facts to 18

Add to solve the problems in the problem list. Then, find the same problems in the puzzle. Circle the hidden problems and write + and = in the correct places. Problems are hidden across and down.

8 + 7 = 15   9 + 5 = ___   9 + 2 = ___   7 + 3 = ___   4 + 6 = ___

6 + 7 = ___   7 + 6 = ___   5 + 5 = ___   9 + 9 = ___   8 + 6 = ___

7 + 4 = ___   5 + 9 = ___   8 + 8 = ___   6 + 5 = ___   2 + 8 = ___

9 + 8 = ___   6 + 9 = ___

4 + 8 = ___   6 + 6 = ___

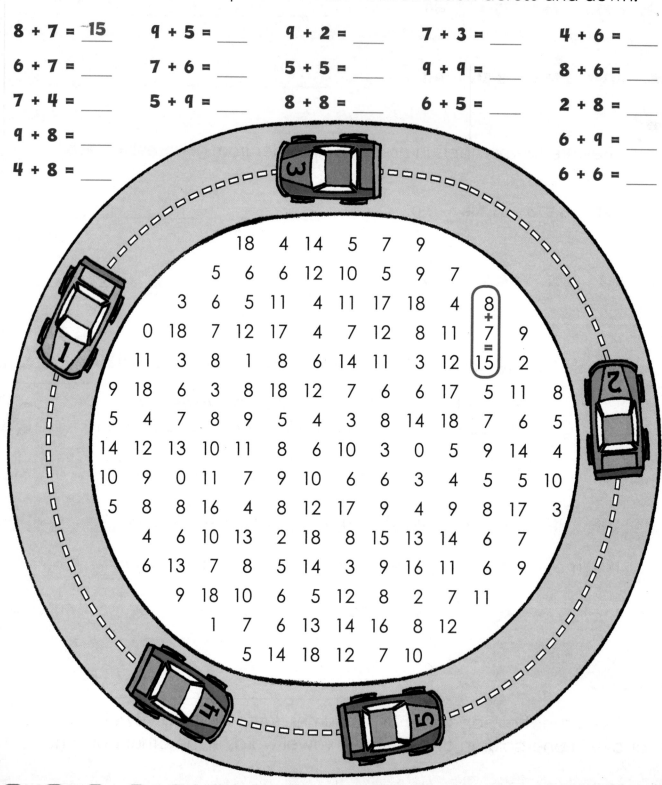

Silent e

A **silent e** at the end of a word makes the first vowel have a long sound.
Say the words and listen to the vowel sounds.

glāze   thēse   shīne   tōte   fūme

Read each word and circle the long vowel sound. Underline the silent e.

1. doze
2. brave
3. wipe
4. poke
5. thrive
6. late
7. trade

8. rise
9. tone
10. joke
11. mode
12. tile
13. twice
14. game

15. these
16. stove
17. bone
18. blame
19. side
20. kite
21. mate

Expanded Notation

Look at the key and the model for a three-digit number.
Then, fill in the missing information below.

Key
0 = hundreds
/ = tens
• = ones

Standard number: 482
Expanded notation: 400 + 80 + 2
Pictorial model: 0000 ///////// ••

A. Standard number	Expanded notation	Pictorial model
327		

B. Standard number	Expanded notation	Pictorial model
	200 + 50 + 4	

C. Standard number	Expanded notation	Pictorial model
		00000000 //// •••••

Fiction or Nonfiction?

Stories can be divided into two different types. **Fiction** is drawn from the imagination, and the events and characters are not real. **Nonfiction** has only facts about people, places, subjects, and events that are real.

Read the following paragraph and write **fiction** or **nonfiction** in the box.

Army ants are some of the most feared types of ants. These ants are very destructive and can eat all living things in their paths. Army ants travel at night in groups of hundreds of thousands through the tropical forests of Africa and South America.

Now write your own story. On the bottom blank line, write whether your story is **fiction** or **nonfiction**.

_____

_____

_____

_____

_____

_____

_____

_____

Try to think of a story character you would like to be. Draw a picture of yourself as this new character.

Subtraction Facts to 18

Subtract to solve the problems in the problem lists. Then, find the same problems in the puzzle. Circle each problem and write – and = in the correct places. Problems are hidden across and down.

```
          2   8  19   0  11   4   6
       7  8   0  13  12   1   7   6  16
(11 – 5 = 6) 9 16   8   1   0  12   4   9   8   1
    4 14   5   1   6   0   5   8   4   8   2   2   5  12  10
    9 19   7   3  13   6   1   0   5   4  14   7   6   7  17
   14  4   2   2   5   0  16   7   9   7  18   6   2   5  10
   10  0   6   3   0   7   8  14   3  10   1  18   9  13   5
    8  5  11   8   3  18  10   7   3   2   7  11   4   7   7
    2  3   9  14  16   6   4  12  11  19   9   8   0   9  15
    7  1   5  16   7   0  10  17   8   2  13  15   8   7  12
    9  0  11   5   7   9   6  12  15   7   8  18  14   4   9
    2  8  17   0   8  10   7   4  11   6   0   1  11   1   3
       7  5  12   2  18   9   9   6   8   9   0
          1   3   8   8   2   5   1   0   1
```

Problem List

11 – 5 = __6__

13 – 8 = _____

12 – 7 = _____

11 – 8 = _____

16 – 7 = _____

15 – 8 = _____

10 – 8 = _____

15 – 7 = _____

5 – 0 = _____

Problem List

10 – 2 = _____

12 – 8 = _____

11 – 4 = _____

10 – 7 = _____

4 – 2 = _____

9 – 2 = _____

6 – 4 = _____

18 – 9 = _____

12 – 9 = _____

Number Sentences

Read each word problem.
Circle the number sentence that shows the correct answer.

A. Brian solved two difficult math problems. It took him 11 minutes to complete the first problem and 13 minutes to complete the second. How long did it take him to complete both problems?

11 + 2 = 13   11 + 13 = 24

13 − 11 = 2   11 + 2 = 13

B. Mary invited 25 friends to her birthday party, but only 17 showed up. How many of the invited friends did not come?

17 + 25 = 43   43 − 25 = 17

25 − 17 = 8   17 − 8 = 9

C. Sharon has already read 12 pages in her science book this evening. If she has to read 18 more pages tonight, how many pages was her reading assignment for tonight?

12 + 6 = 18   18 +-12 = 30

30 + 12 = 42   18 − 6 = 12

Y as a Vowel

The letter **y** at the end of a word can make the
long e sound or the **long i** sound.
Write each word from the word list in the correct column.

Word List

hurry
spy
fry
party
by
busy
lazy
try

1. y = $\bar{e}$ sound

_____

_____

_____

_____

2. y = $\bar{i}$ sound

_____

_____

_____

_____

Schwa Sound (ə)

Some vowels do not make a long or short sound.
These vowels make the **schwa** sound.
The symbol ə means a vowel makes a schwa sound.

Say the words. Listen to the schwa sound (ə) in each.

sofa (sofə)   lemon (lemən)   father (fathər)

For each pair of words, underline the schwa symbol in the first word.
Circle the vowel that makes the schwa sound in the second word.

1. systəm   s y s t e m   **2.** circəs   c i r c u s   **3.** əbout   a b o u t

4. forwərd   f o r w a r d   **5.** robən   r o b i n   **6.** aprən   a p r o n

7. chorəs   c h o r u s   **8.** camerə   c a m e r a   **9.** pencəl   p e n c i l

10. lettər   l e t t e r   **11.** ovər   o v e r   **12.** campər   c a m p e r

Story Problems

Read each word problem and circle the correct answer.
Use extra paper to help solve the problems if you need it.

A. Marcia will run every day next week. If she runs
1 mile on Sunday, 3 miles on Monday, and
5 miles on Tuesday, how many miles will she run
on Wednesday?

9   11

7   13

B. John and Tonya went to the store to buy 2 boxes
of oatmeal cookies. Each box has 12 cookies.
How many cookies will John and Tonya have?

24   36

48   16

C. Alex has 23 marbles. If Alex has 4 friends and he
gives each friend a marble, how many marbles
will Alex have left?

27   19

4   20

Reading and Writing Numbers

A number is usually written using digits in the appropriate place value spots. This is called **standard form**.

Examples: five thousand, two hundred, fifty-one = **5,251**

twenty-two thousand, thirty-three = **22,033**

Write each number in standard form on the line.

A. six hundred thirty-four = _____

B. eight thousand, two hundred fifty-one = _____

C. nine thousand, three hundred twenty-two = _____

D. twenty-seven thousand, eight hundred = _____

E. seventy thousand, one hundred two = _____

F. eighty-three thousand, three hundred eleven = _____

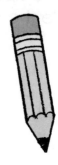

Beginning Blends: bl, cl, fl

Write each word in the correct column.

| flute | blue | clean | clasp | float | fleet | blimp | blink | cloak |

bl	cl	fl
_____	_____	_____
_____	_____	_____
_____	_____	_____

Expanded Notation

Expanded notation is writing a number to show the value of each digit in the number.   **Examples:**   583 = **500 + 80 + 3**

six hundred fifty-two = **600 + 50 + 2**

Circle the letter beside the correct expanded notation for each number.

Eight hundred seventy-five =

A. 8,000 + 70 + 5

B. 800 + 70 + 5

C. 80,000 + 700 +50

D. 800,000 + 70 + 5

Six thousand forty-eight =

A. 6,000 + 400 + 80

B. 10,000 + 6,000 + 400 + 80

C. 6,000 + 40 + 8

D. 60,000 + 40 + 8

Beginning Blends: gl, pl, sl

Say the word that names each picture.
Circle the beginning blend of each word.

1.

gl

pl

sl

2.

gl

pl

sl

3.

gl

pl

sl

4.

gl

pl

sl

5.

gl

pl

sl

6.

gl

pl

sl

Nouns

Common nouns name any one of a group of things.
Proper nouns name a specific person, place, or thing.

Each sentence has one common noun and one proper noun. Write the common noun to the left of the sentence and the proper noun to the right.

Common Nouns

_____

_____

_____

_____

_____

_____

_____

_____

My cousin lives in Spain.

Smokey is a famous bear.

My family ate at Pizza Barn.

Ogden is a beautiful city.

Isaac Newton was a scientist.

The first satellite was Sputnik I.

George Eastman made cameras.

The Pilgrims sailed for two months.

Proper Nouns

_____

_____

_____

_____

_____

_____

_____

_____

Comparing Numbers

Study the examples below. To compare each pair of numbers, use less than (<), greater than (>), or equal to (=). Write the correct symbol in each oval.

Examples: 375 (<) 6,200   7,000 (=) 7,000   3,482 (>) 2,843

A. 620 ( ) 6,200

B. 493 ( ) 439

C. 6,432 ( ) 16,408

D. 9,286 ( ) 13,489

E. 724 ( ) 724

F. 3,080 ( ) 3,800

G. 45,015 ( ) 45,016

H. 397,124 ( ) 387,425

I. 488,188 ( ) 488,018

Two-Digit Addition with Regrouping

Add to solve the problems.

A.
$$54 + 26$$

B.
$$44 + 39$$

C.
$$19 + 76$$

D.
$$24 + 47$$

E.
$$38 + 57$$

F.
$$29 + 64$$

G.
$$49 + 31$$

H.
$$78 + 12$$

I.
$$36 + 46$$

Beginning Blends: br, cr, dr, fr

Say the name of each picture. Fill in the circle if
the word begins with the blend in the box.

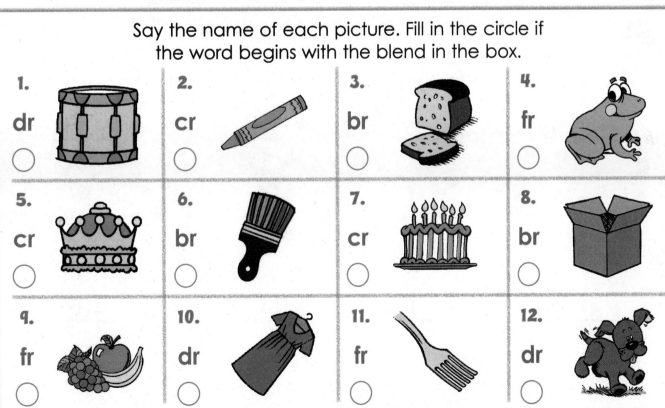

1. dr ◯

2. cr ◯

3. br ◯

4. fr ◯

5. cr ◯

6. br ◯

7. cr ◯

8. br ◯

9. fr ◯

10. dr ◯

11. fr ◯

12. dr ◯

Beginning Blends: gr, pr, tr

Say the names of the pictures.
Circle the picture that begins with each blend shown.

1.
gr

2.
pr

3.
tr

Read each word. Circle the beginning blend **gr**, **pr**, or **tr** in each word.

4. preview	**5.** produce	**6.** truly	**7.** triumph
8. tread	**9.** prop	**10.** tree	**11.** predict
12. grew	**13.** ground	**14.** gruel	**15.** grant

Two-Digit Subtraction with Regrouping

Subtract to solve the problems.

A.
$$70 - 19$$

B.
$$82 - 17$$

C.
$$70 - 22$$

D.
$$90 - 79$$

E.
$$78 - 59$$

F.
$$53 - 14$$

G.
$$66 - 8$$

H.
$$54 - 38$$

Pronouns

Circle the **pronoun** that completes each sentence.

1. _____ grew corn and tomatoes in his garden.

    Him   His   He

2. Please tell _____ what vegetables you would like to plant this year.

    we   mine   us

3. Tisha and _____ love to plant our watermelon seeds.

    we   I   us

4. Mother wants to plant flowers in her garden so that _____ will have something special.

    us   mine   she

5. We plant carrots, lettuce, and beans because _____ are good to eat.

    they   them   she

Addition with Regrouping

Math

A. $\begin{array}{r} 35 \\ + 27 \\ \hline \end{array}$	**B.** $\begin{array}{r} 85 \\ + 56 \\ \hline \end{array}$	**C.** $\begin{array}{r} 28 \\ + 14 \\ \hline \end{array}$	**D.** $\begin{array}{r} 78 \\ + 66 \\ \hline \end{array}$
E. $\begin{array}{r} 348 \\ + 235 \\ \hline \end{array}$	**F.** $\begin{array}{r} 628 \\ + 597 \\ \hline \end{array}$	**G.** $\begin{array}{r} 565 \\ + 217 \\ \hline \end{array}$	**H.** $\begin{array}{r} 4,188 \\ + 176 \\ \hline \end{array}$

Adding Two or More Addends

Keep the place values lined up to find the right sum. Solve the problems.

A.
```
   62
 + 27
```

B.
```
   75
 + 85
```

C.
```
   54
 + 92
```

D.
```
   736
    89
 + 104
```

E.
```
   3,482
     437
 +    68
```

F.
```
   246
   442
 +  53
```

G.
```
   6,428
   1,375
 + 3,684
```

H.
```
   30,147
   25,236
 + 42,613
```

I.
```
   2,804
   1,366
 + 5,391
```

J.
```
   5,894
   1,388
 + 3,137
```

K.
```
   28,123
   33,294
 + 46,510
```

L.
```
   14,738
   22,856
 + 17,979
```

Beginning Blends: sk, sm, sn, sp

Say the name of each picture. Circle the word that
names the picture and write its beginning blend.

1.

smell
spoon
skill

2.

smoke
spy
snack

3.

skunk
snowman
snare

4.

smear
spore
skate

5.

smack
skirt
sniff

6.

spool
skit
snoop

7.

smile
sneak
spoof

8.

skull
spill
snail

30

Action Verbs

An **action verb** tells what the subject of a sentence does.
Look at the action verbs in the following sentences.

Dino plays football in the fall.   **We walk home every day.**

Underline the **action verb** in each sentence.

1. Small airplanes fly over our house every afternoon at 5:00.

2. The rooster on our farm crows every morning at 6:00.

3. My dad plows the fields near our house in the spring.

4. The ducks in the pond splash water everywhere each afternoon.

5. Mother feeds the chickens twice a day.

6. My brother and I clean the barn every Saturday.

Two-Digit Subtraction

Math

Subtract to solve the problems.

A.	B.	C.	D.
17 − 16	46 − 25	84 − 53	78 − 16
E.	F.	G.	H.
25 − 14	27 − 13	75 − 31	68 − 14
I.	J.	K.	L.
23 − 12	42 − 31	24 − 13	82 − 71

Large Number Subtraction

Solve the problems.

A. 52 −39	**B.** 47 −19	**C.** 61 −25	**D.** 980 −430
E. 543 −298	**F.** 766 −384	**G.** 7,303 −3,855	**H.** 8,624 −4,937
I. 5,322 −1,404	**J.** 49,718 −32,579	**K.** 38,972 −24,687	**L.** 15,476 −13,287

Correct Spellings

Look at the words in each row. Circle the **correctly spelled** word.

1. buzes   buzzes   buzzis
2. schol   schoul   school
3. sumtim   sometime   sometme
4. baloon   balloon   ballon
5. work   wrok   werk
6. monoy   money   monie
7. chaneg   chang   change
8. reding   raeding   reading
9. homework   homwork   homewrok

Multiplication Tables for Basic Facts 0-9

Glue these tables onto index cards and use them to practice your facts.

0

0 x 0 = 0	0 x 5 = 0
0 x 1 = 0	0 x 6 = 0
0 x 2 = 0	0 x 7 = 0
0 x 3 = 0	0 x 8 = 0
0 x 4 = 0	0 x 9 = 0

5

5 x 0 = 0	5 x 5 = 25
5 x 1 = 5	5 x 6 = 30
5 x 2 = 10	5 x 7 = 35
5 x 3 = 15	5 x 8 = 40
5 x 4 = 20	5 x 9 = 45

1

1 x 0 = 0	1 x 5 = 5
1 x 1 = 1	1 x 6 = 6
1 x 2 = 2	1 x 7 = 7
1 x 3 = 3	1 x 8 = 8
1 x 4 = 4	1 x 9 = 9

6

6 x 0 = 0	6 x 5 = 30
6 x 1 = 6	6 x 6 = 36
6 x 2 = 12	6 x 7 = 42
6 x 3 = 18	6 x 8 = 48
6 x 4 = 24	6 x 9 = 54

2

2 x 0 = 0	2 x 5 = 10
2 x 1 = 2	2 x 6 = 12
2 x 2 = 4	2 x 7 = 14
2 x 3 = 6	2 x 8 = 16
2 x 4 = 8	2 x 9 = 18

7

7 x 0 = 0	7 x 5 = 35
7 x 1 = 7	7 x 6 = 42
7 x 2 = 14	7 x 7 = 49
7 x 3 = 21	7 x 8 = 56
7 x 4 = 28	7 x 9 = 63

3

3 x 0 = 0	3 x 5 = 15
3 x 1 = 3	3 x 6 = 18
3 x 2 = 6	3 x 7 = 21
3 x 3 = 9	3 x 8 = 24
3 x 4 = 12	3 x 9 = 27

8

8 x 0 = 0	8 x 5 = 40
8 x 1 = 8	8 x 6 = 48
8 x 2 = 16	8 x 7 = 56
8 x 3 = 24	8 x 8 = 64
8 x 4 = 32	8 x 9 = 72

4

4 x 0 = 0	4 x 5 = 20
4 x 1 = 4	4 x 6 = 24
4 x 2 = 8	4 x 7 = 28
4 x 3 = 12	4 x 8 = 32
4 x 4 = 16	4 x 9 = 36

9

9 x 0 = 0	9 x 5 = 45
9 x 1 = 9	9 x 6 = 54
9 x 2 = 18	9 x 7 = 63
9 x 3 = 27	9 x 8 = 72
9 x 4 = 36	9 x 9 = 81

Syllables

Answer the questions. Write the answers on the lines.

newt

hip•po•pot•a•mus

star•fish
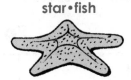

en•cy•clo•pe•di•a

ta•ran•tu•la

zuc•chi•ni

1. Which word has five syllables? _____

2. How many syllables does **encyclopedia** have? _____

3. Which word has three syllables? _____

4. How many syllables does **starfish** have? _____

5. Which word has one syllable? _____

6. How many syllables does **tarantula** have? _____

Multiplication Facts for 0

When the number **0** is a factor, the product is always **0**.

$$3 \times 0 = 0 \qquad 0 \times 9 = 0$$

Complete the facts for 0.

0 × 0 = ____   0 × 5 = ____

0 × 1 = ____   0 × 6 = ____

0 × 2 = ____   0 × 7 = ____

0 × 3 = ____   0 × 8 = ____

0 × 4 = ____   0 × 9 = ____

Pictograph

The following **pictograph** shows the favorite pets of students in Mrs. Mill's third grade class. Each picture stands for one student's vote.

Favorite Pets

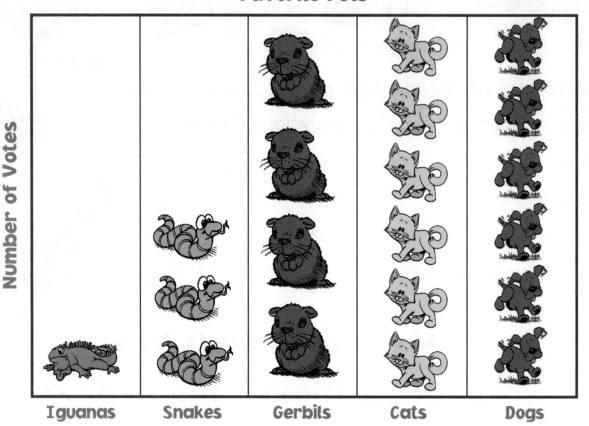

Look at the graph and answer the questions.

A. How many children voted for gerbils? _____

B. What pet received the fewest votes? _____

C. How many more votes did cats receive than snakes? _____

D. How many children voted in all? _____

E. Which two pets were equally popular? _____

_____

Multiplication Facts for 1

When the number **1** is a factor, the product equals the other factor.

$$1 \times 9 = 9 \qquad 2 \times 1 = 2$$

Complete the facts for 1.

1 X 0 = ___   1 X 5 = ___

1 X 1 = ___   1 X 6 = ___

1 X 2 = ___   1 X 7 = ___

1 X 3 = ___   1 X 8 = ___

1 X 4 = ___   1 X 9 = ___

Beginning Blends: st, sw, tw

Say each word below. If the word begins with the **st** blend, circle it.
If the word begins with the **sw** blend, draw an **X** on it.
If the word begins with the **tw** blend, underline it.

1. twelve   2. staple   3. twist   4. tweak   5. swan   6. stand

7. swat   8. swipe   9. sting   10. sweep   11. twilight   12. stare

Say the name of each picture. Write the two letters that
make up the word's beginning blend.

13.    **14.**    **15.**    **16.**    **17.**    **18.**

Beginning Blends: scr, spl, spr, str

Circle the **beginning blend** in each word below.

1. scratch   2. stride   3. sprinkle   4. spruce   5. splay
6. sprig   7. split   8. scribble   9. straight   10. street
11. splurge   12. scroll   13. stream   14. spray   15. sprig

Use the beginning blend **scr**, **spl**, **spr**, or **str**
to complete the name of each picture.

 16. _____ub
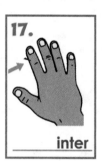 17. _____inter
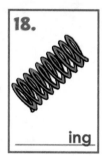 18. _____ing
 19. _____eam
 20. _____oller
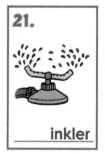 21. _____inkler

Multiplication Facts for 2

Multiply to solve the problems.

A. 3 ×2   B. 8 ×2   C. 0 ×2   D. 2 ×6

E. 2 ×5   F. 2 ×7   G. 4 ×2   H. 2 ×2

I. 2 ×9   J. 1 ×2   K. 2 ×8   L. 2 ×5

Story Webs

Complete the story web. Use the words in the web to write a story. Be sure to use capital letters and periods. Think of a title for your story.

Things to Think About

Who is this story about?

Where does this story take place?

How does this story begin?

What happens next?

How will this story end?

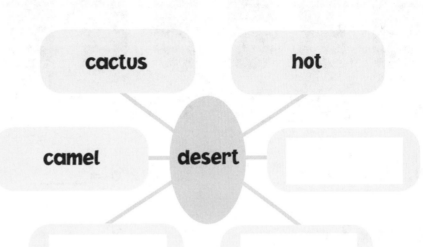

Multiplication Facts for 3

Use the sets below to help complete the multiplication facts.

A. 1 x 3 = _____

B. 9 x 3 = _____

C. 4 x 3 = _____

D. 5 x 3 = _____

E. 6 x 3 = _____

F. 2 x 3 = _____

G. 3 x 3 = _____

H. 7 x 3 = _____

I. 8 x 3 = _____

J. 0 x 3 = _____

K. 3 x 9 = _____

L. 3 x 3 = _____

Vowel Sound ai/ay

Write a word from the word list under each picture.

Word List   waist   ray   crayon   paint   hay   train

1.

_____

2.

_____

3.

_____

4.

_____

5.

_____

6.

_____

Remove pages 41–44. Cut along dashed lines. Staple pages in order.

Word Searches

1

Parties!

Circle the words from the word list in the puzzle below.

Word List

party
celebrate
birthday
decorate
special
excited
surprise
invite
ribbon
balloon

```
I C R I B B O N T E
N E B L E S Y A M X
A L S I N V I T E C
D E C O R A T E U I
E B J E F T G R M T
C R C S U R H E A E
B A L L O O N D H D
I T N S P E C I A L
R E X I C P A R T Y
T R S U R P R I S E
```

3

Success!

Circle the words from the word list in the puzzle below.

```
B A R E M T A D H S
L W A D M I R E S T
D A C H I E V E P U
S R B L O A C D O D
P D I R S C F M T E
E U Q B U T L I L N
C T X S B A S R I T
I S H I K O D A G S
A D O W B S N X H C
L P R E F F O R T M
```

2

Sports

Circle the words from the word list in the puzzle below.

```
F D R O M A S C O T
I S A U N I F O R M
A C P S D G U M F A
L H E O T E M P E L
D A H P R S H E M G
W M S L N T R T U D
H P G A M E S E L X
U I D Y F J H E O K
Y O V E R T I M E H
S N R R E F U N A P
```

4

42

Bath Time

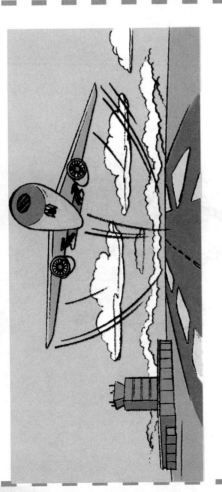

Circle the words from the word list in the puzzle below.

5

Word List

bathtub
bubbles
soap
clean
water
lather
splash
towel
scrub
washcloth

```
S J D R E K E L O R
I P H S G C W P N X
B C L E A N A R P Y
K A A P O C H V O
W S T O S W A T E R
N C H H K H G O S F
C R E I T R A W T E
P U R P V U V E U N
S B E B U B B L E S
D W A S H C L O T H
```

Air Travel

Circle the words from the word list in the puzzle below.

7

Word List

airplane
pilot
baggage
cabin
ticket
landing
depart
flight
hangar
tower

```
M E T I C K E T I H
N O W A N D R L W D
F L I G H T F I R E
E A B V T A K B N P
L N R U O J N A E A
P D I T W U L G E R
F I R H E P R G A T
A N K S R D N A R R
W G P I L O T G W E
T C A B I N S E L V
```

Farming

Circle the words from the word list in the puzzle below.

```
L J U T N E P M J S
I S H O R S E S F O
V B I B X A S D E Q
E H A L U P C I R U
S A W R O O S T E R
T R E R N G N B O K
O V C A H Y C T H R
C E V X S T A B L E
K S F A R M E R P W
G T N E Y D R A D S
```

6

Word List

farmer
tractor
crops
rooster
horses
stable
barnyard
livestock
harvest
silo

Bicycles

Circle the words from the word list in the puzzle below.

```
W H E A C I W P N O
P K P E D K H A E P
B I C Y C L E R D A
R C B O R S E A T A
I K L F P I L P E H
E S O P A J D M A T
H A N D L E B A R B
D T L E T S L E X K
S N K A H C H A I N
E D B L T R P O G L
```

8

Word List

bicycle
seat
rider
chain
wheel
path
handlebar
pedal
kickstand
park
helmet
lock

Punctuation Marks

Each sentence below is missing a punctuation mark.
Put the correct **punctuation mark** in each place that needs one.

1. Mario had a hamburger, some potatoes, and a milk shake for dinner. He can t eat another bite!

2. Mr. and Mrs Blair went to the movies last night with their three children.

3. Did you know that Maple Ave. crosses Second St at Main?

4. Dr. Barnes was able to see Mark yesterday afternoon

5. José and Latasha visited Maine, Vermont New York, and New Hampshire this past summer.

6. Is New York abbreviated NJ, NC, or NY

7. Don hit two home runs in the game. His team won

8. Wow What a neat costume! I wish I were a pirate!

9. Benita thinks that she would like to be a doctor but she also thinks that she may become a teacher.

10. Bernie s favorite ice-cream flavors are chocolate, vanilla, butter pecan, and maple nut.

Vowel Sound ee/ea

Complete each word by writing the letters **ee** or **ea** on the line.

1. wh _____ l
2. ind _____ d
3. cl _____ n

4. l _____ ve
5. sp _____ k
6. sn _____ ze

7. tr _____ t
8. sl _____ p
9. s _____ n

10. b _____ p
11. sl _____ t
12. tr _____

13. dr _____ m
14. str _____ t
15. gr _____ se

BONUS Write **ee** or **ea** to make each word match the clue.

st _____ l
(hard metal)

p _____ k
(to look)

w _____ k
(not strong)

Multiplication Facts for 4

When a number is multiplied by 4, it is the same as
adding the number to itself 4 times.

4 x 3 = 12   is the same as   3 + 3 + 3 + 3 = 12

Complete the facts for 4.

4 x 0 = ___   4 x 5 = ___

4 x 1 = ___   4 x 6 = ___

4 x 2 = ___   4 x 7 = ___

4 x 3 = ___   4 x 8 = ___

4 x 4 = ___   4 x 9 = ___

Multiplication Facts for 5

Use the sets of 5 below to help complete the multiplication facts.

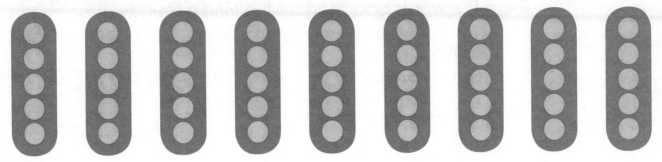

A. 4 x 5 = _____

B. 4 x 5 = _____

C. 8 x 5 = _____

D. 7 x 5 = _____

E. 2 x 5 = _____

F. 9 x 5 = _____

G. 3 x 5 = _____

H. 6 x 5 = _____

I. 1 x 5 = _____

Vowel Sound oa

Phonics

Use the words from the word list to complete each sentence.
Circle the **long o** sound of **oa** in each word.

Word List

loan
afloat
coach
oak
toaster
coast

1. Mr. Collins is our basketball _____.

2. The acorns fell from the _____ tree.

3. We hoped our raft would stay _____ in the water.

4. The storm hit the Florida _____ last night.

5. Mindy asked if I would _____ her my bike.

6. Put the bread in the _____, then butter it.

Complete each word by writing the letters **oa**. Read the word and listen for the **long o** sound.

7. r____d   8. c____l   9. t____d

10. g____t   11. l____d   12. b____t

13. s____p   14. g____l   15. ____ts

Vowel Sound ue/ui

Complete each word by writing **ue** or **ui** on the line.
Read the words and listen for the **long u** sound.

1. s_____t

2. cr_____l

3. s_____

4. fr_____t

5. br_____se

6. f_____l

7. tr_____

8. d_____

9. d_____l

10. n_____sance

11. cr_____se

12. j_____ce

13. cl_____

14. gl_____

15. T_____sday

Logical Thinking

Read the following word problems. Make notes to help you find the
order of the people in each problem. Circle the correct answer.

A. Four marathon runners ran in a race. Use the clues to determine the winner.

> Mario ran faster than Shane.
>
> Shane ran faster than Randy.
>
> Tyler ran faster than Mario.

Who won the race?

a. Mario   c. Shane

b. Randy   d. Tyler

B. Davis lined up his four sisters by height. Use the clues below to determine the order of the sisters.

> Sally is taller than Kendra.
>
> Mary is the tallest sister.
>
> Trisha is not as tall as Kendra.

In what order did the sisters stand?

a. Mary, Trisha, Kendra, Sally
b. Mary, Sally, Trisha, Kendra
c. Mary, Sally, Kendra, Trisha
d. Sally, Mary, Trisha, Kendra

Main Idea

A paragraph is a group of detail sentences that support a **main idea**. The main idea is usually in the topic sentence at the beginning of the paragraph.

Look at each paragraph below and circle the main idea. Underline the detail sentence that does **not** support the main idea.

1. Yesterday my class visited the zoo. We were amazed at all the animals that lived there. There were animals from all over the world in their natural habitats. I live in a house. My favorite animal was the elephant who lived on the African plains.

2. We played a game in our classroom yesterday called Silent Ball. To play this game everyone must stand in a circle and be absolutely silent. A sponge ball is then passed from person to person. The ball may be passed to a person next to you or to a person across the room. Mary does not like the game, so she chose not to play. If a player misses the ball or makes a sound, he must sit down. The last person standing is the winner of this soundless game.

3. José has an unusual pet. It is an iguana named Pete. Pete lives in a glass house made from an old fish aquarium. He eats a special diet of fruit and green plants. Sleeping at night and being active during the day is Pete's normal routine. My friend Martin has an iguana at his house, too. Pete has a greenish gray appearance and blends into his environment. Jose's unusual pet is fun to observe.

Beat the Clock (Multiplication Facts to 5)

A.
$$\begin{array}{r} 4 \\ \times\,3 \\ \hline \end{array} \quad \begin{array}{r} 3 \\ \times\,1 \\ \hline \end{array} \quad \begin{array}{r} 2 \\ \times\,2 \\ \hline \end{array} \quad \begin{array}{r} 5 \\ \times\,5 \\ \hline \end{array} \quad \begin{array}{r} 3 \\ \times\,5 \\ \hline \end{array} \quad \begin{array}{r} 0 \\ \times\,3 \\ \hline \end{array} \quad \begin{array}{r} 4 \\ \times\,2 \\ \hline \end{array} \quad \begin{array}{r} 1 \\ \times\,4 \\ \hline \end{array} \quad \begin{array}{r} 2 \\ \times\,0 \\ \hline \end{array} \quad \begin{array}{r} 5 \\ \times\,2 \\ \hline \end{array}$$

B.
$$\begin{array}{r} 5 \\ \times\,5 \\ \hline \end{array} \quad \begin{array}{r} 4 \\ \times\,2 \\ \hline \end{array} \quad \begin{array}{r} 0 \\ \times\,5 \\ \hline \end{array} \quad \begin{array}{r} 4 \\ \times\,4 \\ \hline \end{array} \quad \begin{array}{r} 1 \\ \times\,5 \\ \hline \end{array} \quad \begin{array}{r} 2 \\ \times\,3 \\ \hline \end{array} \quad \begin{array}{r} 5 \\ \times\,4 \\ \hline \end{array} \quad \begin{array}{r} 2 \\ \times\,5 \\ \hline \end{array} \quad \begin{array}{r} 0 \\ \times\,1 \\ \hline \end{array} \quad \begin{array}{r} 3 \\ \times\,3 \\ \hline \end{array}$$

C.
$$\begin{array}{r} 0 \\ \times\,2 \\ \hline \end{array} \quad \begin{array}{r} 3 \\ \times\,1 \\ \hline \end{array} \quad \begin{array}{r} 5 \\ \times\,1 \\ \hline \end{array} \quad \begin{array}{r} 4 \\ \times\,5 \\ \hline \end{array} \quad \begin{array}{r} 3 \\ \times\,0 \\ \hline \end{array} \quad \begin{array}{r} 1 \\ \times\,1 \\ \hline \end{array} \quad \begin{array}{r} 2 \\ \times\,2 \\ \hline \end{array} \quad \begin{array}{r} 0 \\ \times\,1 \\ \hline \end{array} \quad \begin{array}{r} 4 \\ \times\,0 \\ \hline \end{array} \quad \begin{array}{r} 1 \\ \times\,2 \\ \hline \end{array}$$

D.
$$\begin{array}{r} 2 \\ \times\,3 \\ \hline \end{array} \quad \begin{array}{r} 3 \\ \times\,4 \\ \hline \end{array} \quad \begin{array}{r} 2 \\ \times\,0 \\ \hline \end{array} \quad \begin{array}{r} 5 \\ \times\,3 \\ \hline \end{array} \quad \begin{array}{r} 2 \\ \times\,5 \\ \hline \end{array} \quad \begin{array}{r} 4 \\ \times\,4 \\ \hline \end{array} \quad \begin{array}{r} 0 \\ \times\,0 \\ \hline \end{array} \quad \begin{array}{r} 3 \\ \times\,1 \\ \hline \end{array} \quad \begin{array}{r} 5 \\ \times\,2 \\ \hline \end{array} \quad \begin{array}{r} 1 \\ \times\,2 \\ \hline \end{array}$$

E.
$$\begin{array}{r} 5 \\ \times\,0 \\ \hline \end{array} \quad \begin{array}{r} 1 \\ \times\,3 \\ \hline \end{array} \quad \begin{array}{r} 2 \\ \times\,1 \\ \hline \end{array} \quad \begin{array}{r} 3 \\ \times\,2 \\ \hline \end{array} \quad \begin{array}{r} 0 \\ \times\,2 \\ \hline \end{array} \quad \begin{array}{r} 4 \\ \times\,1 \\ \hline \end{array} \quad \begin{array}{r} 3 \\ \times\,4 \\ \hline \end{array} \quad \begin{array}{r} 1 \\ \times\,0 \\ \hline \end{array} \quad \begin{array}{r} 3 \\ \times\,5 \\ \hline \end{array} \quad \begin{array}{r} 5 \\ \times\,1 \\ \hline \end{array}$$

F.
$$\begin{array}{r} 2 \\ \times\,4 \\ \hline \end{array} \quad \begin{array}{r} 0 \\ \times\,5 \\ \hline \end{array} \quad \begin{array}{r} 0 \\ \times\,0 \\ \hline \end{array} \quad \begin{array}{r} 4 \\ \times\,2 \\ \hline \end{array} \quad \begin{array}{r} 3 \\ \times\,3 \\ \hline \end{array} \quad \begin{array}{r} 1 \\ \times\,5 \\ \hline \end{array} \quad \begin{array}{r} 1 \\ \times\,1 \\ \hline \end{array} \quad \begin{array}{r} 4 \\ \times\,1 \\ \hline \end{array} \quad \begin{array}{r} 3 \\ \times\,0 \\ \hline \end{array} \quad \begin{array}{r} 0 \\ \times\,4 \\ \hline \end{array}$$

G.
$$\begin{array}{r} 5 \\ \times\,4 \\ \hline \end{array} \quad \begin{array}{r} 2 \\ \times\,1 \\ \hline \end{array} \quad \begin{array}{r} 0 \\ \times\,0 \\ \hline \end{array} \quad \begin{array}{r} 1 \\ \times\,5 \\ \hline \end{array} \quad \begin{array}{r} 5 \\ \times\,0 \\ \hline \end{array} \quad \begin{array}{r} 4 \\ \times\,4 \\ \hline \end{array} \quad \begin{array}{r} 1 \\ \times\,2 \\ \hline \end{array} \quad \begin{array}{r} 2 \\ \times\,5 \\ \hline \end{array} \quad \begin{array}{r} 5 \\ \times\,1 \\ \hline \end{array} \quad \begin{array}{r} 2 \\ \times\,4 \\ \hline \end{array}$$

H.
$$\begin{array}{r} 4 \\ \times\,0 \\ \hline \end{array} \quad \begin{array}{r} 5 \\ \times\,2 \\ \hline \end{array} \quad \begin{array}{r} 1 \\ \times\,4 \\ \hline \end{array} \quad \begin{array}{r} 3 \\ \times\,0 \\ \hline \end{array} \quad \begin{array}{r} 3 \\ \times\,2 \\ \hline \end{array} \quad \begin{array}{r} 1 \\ \times\,3 \\ \hline \end{array} \quad \begin{array}{r} 5 \\ \times\,3 \\ \hline \end{array} \quad \begin{array}{r} 0 \\ \times\,1 \\ \hline \end{array} \quad \begin{array}{r} 2 \\ \times\,2 \\ \hline \end{array} \quad \begin{array}{r} 4 \\ \times\,3 \\ \hline \end{array}$$

I.
$$\begin{array}{r} 4 \\ \times\,5 \\ \hline \end{array} \quad \begin{array}{r} 0 \\ \times\,3 \\ \hline \end{array} \quad \begin{array}{r} 3 \\ \times\,2 \\ \hline \end{array} \quad \begin{array}{r} 4 \\ \times\,3 \\ \hline \end{array} \quad \begin{array}{r} 1 \\ \times\,1 \\ \hline \end{array} \quad \begin{array}{r} 2 \\ \times\,3 \\ \hline \end{array} \quad \begin{array}{r} 3 \\ \times\,5 \\ \hline \end{array} \quad \begin{array}{r} 2 \\ \times\,1 \\ \hline \end{array} \quad \begin{array}{r} 1 \\ \times\,4 \\ \hline \end{array} \quad \begin{array}{r} 5 \\ \times\,5 \\ \hline \end{array}$$

J.
$$\begin{array}{r} 3 \\ \times\,4 \\ \hline \end{array} \quad \begin{array}{r} 1 \\ \times\,0 \\ \hline \end{array} \quad \begin{array}{r} 5 \\ \times\,4 \\ \hline \end{array} \quad \begin{array}{r} 4 \\ \times\,1 \\ \hline \end{array} \quad \begin{array}{r} 5 \\ \times\,3 \\ \hline \end{array} \quad \begin{array}{r} 0 \\ \times\,4 \\ \hline \end{array} \quad \begin{array}{r} 4 \\ \times\,5 \\ \hline \end{array} \quad \begin{array}{r} 1 \\ \times\,3 \\ \hline \end{array} \quad \begin{array}{r} 2 \\ \times\,4 \\ \hline \end{array} \quad \begin{array}{r} 3 \\ \times\,3 \\ \hline \end{array}$$

Time: _____   **Number correct:** _____

Compare and Contrast

Fill in the blanks with words that tell how a cat and dog are alike and different. The first ones have been done for you.

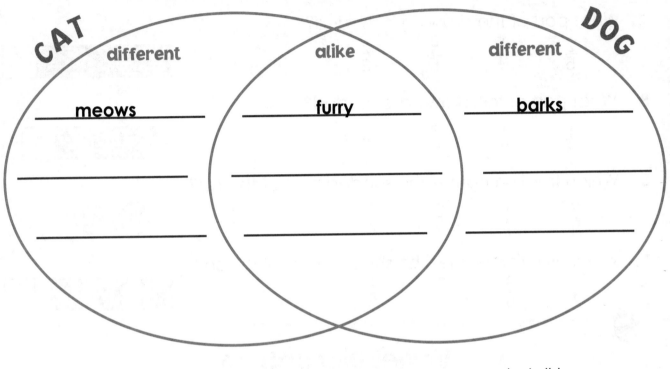

CAT

different

meows

alike

furry

different

barks

DOG

Write two paragraphs below. In the first paragraph, tell how cats and dogs are alike. Tell how each is different in the second paragraph. Give each paragraph a title.

Fractions

Fractions show parts of the whole.

Circle the correct fraction to answer each question.

A. What part of the drawing is shaded?

$\frac{2}{5}$ $\frac{1}{4}$ $\frac{4}{5}$ $\frac{2}{3}$

B. What part of the drawing is shaded?

$\frac{1}{3}$ $\frac{1}{4}$ $\frac{3}{4}$ $\frac{2}{4}$

C. Which fraction names the shaded part of the set?

$\frac{3}{4}$ $\frac{1}{2}$ $\frac{2}{3}$ $\frac{5}{6}$

D. Which fraction names the shaded part of the set?

$\frac{1}{2}$ $\frac{3}{4}$ $\frac{2}{3}$ $\frac{1}{3}$

Vowel Digraph oo

Compare the sound of the letters **oo** in the words **look** and **moon**.
Read each word and circle the matching sound.

$\breve{oo}$ = look $\overline{oo}$ = moon

1. gloomy $\breve{oo}$ $\overline{oo}$ **2.** spooky $\breve{oo}$ $\overline{oo}$ **3.** crook $\breve{oo}$ $\overline{oo}$

4. boot $\breve{oo}$ $\overline{oo}$ **5.** proof $\breve{oo}$ $\overline{oo}$ **6.** rooster $\breve{oo}$ $\overline{oo}$

7. book $\breve{oo}$ $\overline{oo}$ **8.** foolish $\breve{oo}$ $\overline{oo}$ **9.** cook $\breve{oo}$ $\overline{oo}$

10. wool $\breve{oo}$ $\overline{oo}$ **11.** scoop $\breve{oo}$ $\overline{oo}$ **12.** took $\breve{oo}$ $\overline{oo}$

13. stood $\breve{oo}$ $\overline{oo}$ **14.** broom $\breve{oo}$ $\overline{oo}$ **15.** cookie $\breve{oo}$ $\overline{oo}$

Identifying and Using Polygons

Circle the correct answer for each question.

A. Which figure has four sides?

B. Which figure is a triangle?

C. What shape is the top surface of a can of soup?

triangle   square

circle   rectangle

D. Which figure can Roberto build using exactly seven squares?

R-Controlled Sounds: ar, or

Read each sentence. Write the correct word to complete the sentence. Circle the r-controlled vowel.

1. Sam is a good _____, so he shook hands with Mike after the game. (sport spart)

2. Our plane will _____ from the airport at 2:00. (depart deport)

3. Our class will _____ a song in the spring concert. (perform perfarm)

4. My brother and I are taking _____ lessons. (guitor guitar)

5. Ann walks her dog each _____ and afternoon. (morning marning)

6. Rachel is my _____ in the science project. (partner portner)

Symmetry

Symmetry occurs when two halves of a figure match exactly when folded together. The line of symmetry is the location of the fold.

Example: This square shows a **line of symmetry** from top to bottom (vertical).

In each group, circle the figure that has a line of symmetry.

A. 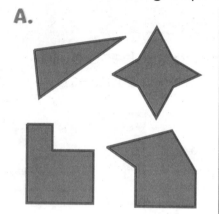 **B.** 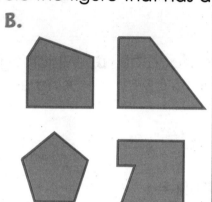 **C.**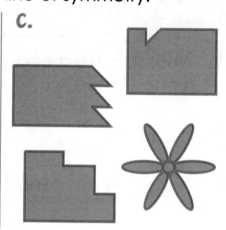

R-Controlled Sounds: er, ir, ur

Choose a word from the word list to complete each sentence.
Circle the letters that make the r-controlled vowel sound.

Word List

first
enter
after
nurse
twirl
purse

1. Please _____ the room quietly.

2. I put the money in my mother's _____.

3. Sally won the _____ place ribbon in the race.

4. The _____ took my temperature.

5. We went to the movies _____ lunch.

6. The ballerina loved to _____.

Circle the letters that make the r-controlled vowel sound in each word.

7. p e r f e c t   8. c u r b   9. r u b b e r   10. n u r s e

11. b r o t h e r   12. u r g e   13. h e r m i t   14. t u r t l e

15. w h i r l   16. p u r s e   17. c u r t a i n   18. p u r p l e

54

Multiplication Facts 0-5

Multiply to solve the problems in the problem list.
Then, find the same problems in the puzzle. Circle the
hidden problems and write **x** and **=** in the correct places.
Problems are hidden across and down.

Problem List

1 x 4 = _4_

5 x 3 = _____

3 x 4 = _____

0 x 3 = _____

4 x 4 = _____

2 x 4 = _____

1 x 2 = _____

5 x 5 = _____

3 x 3 = _____

0 x 1 = _____

4 x 5 = _____

2 x 2 = _____

1 x 1 = _____

5 x 2 = _____

3 x 2 = _____

4 x 2 = _____

4 x 1 = _____

2 x 1 = _____

4 x 3 = _____

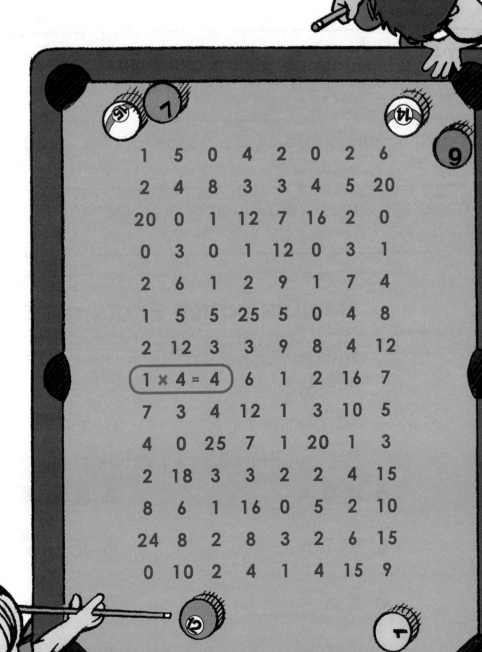

1	5	0	4	2	0	2	6
2	4	8	3	3	4	5	20
20	0	1	12	7	16	2	0
0	3	0	1	12	0	3	1
2	6	1	2	9	1	7	4
1	5	5	25	5	0	4	8
2	12	3	3	9	8	4	12
(1 x 4 = 4)	6	1	2	16	7		
7	3	4	Facts	1	3	10	5
4	0	25	7	1	20	1	3
2	18	3	3	2	2	4	15
8	6	1	16	0	5	2	10
24	8	2	8	3	2	6	15
0	10	2	4	1	4	15	9

New Vocabulary Words

Use a dictionary to help you answer the questions below.
You will have fun learning some new words and interesting facts.
Look up the highlighted words and answer the questions on the lines.

1. Is a **goldfinch** a bag full of gold or a bird?

   _____

2. If you were on a **jetty**, would you be on a jet or a wall along
   a waterfront?

   _____

3. Is a **yak** a long-haired ox or a person that likes to talk?

   _____

4. Would you draw a **parallelogram** or do gymnastics on it?

   _____

Multiplication Facts for 6

When a number is multiplied by 6, it is the
same as adding the number to itself 6 times.

$6 \times 3 = 18$ is the same as $3 + 3 + 3 + 3 + 3 + 3 = 18$

Complete the facts for 6.

$6 \times 0 =$ ___ $6 \times 5 =$ ___

$6 \times 1 =$ ___ $6 \times 6 =$ ___

$6 \times 2 =$ ___ $6 \times 7 =$ ___

$6 \times 3 =$ ___ $6 \times 8 =$ ___

$6 \times 4 =$ ___ $6 \times 9 =$ ___

Understanding What I Read

Read the story. Then, answer the questions.

The Wright Brothers

Orville and Wilbur Wright were famous American brothers. They owned a bicycle shop in Dayton, Ohio. Although they were interested in bicycles, they also loved the idea of flying. In 1896, they began to experiment, or try new ideas, with flight. They started by testing kites and then gliders, which are motorless planes. These tests taught them how an airplane should rise, turn, and come back to earth. The brothers made over 700 glider flights at Kitty Hawk, in North Carolina. This was fun but not good enough for them. Orville and Wilbur put a small engine on a plane they named *Flyer I*. On December 17, 1903, they took the first motor-powered flight that lasted about one minute. The brothers continued to experiment until they could stay in the air for over one hour.

1. What was the main idea of the story? Circle the correct answer.
   a. Testing new ideas is important.
   b. *Flyer I* was the first airplane.
   c. The Wright brothers were early pilots.

2. What does the word **experiment** mean? Circle the correct answer.
   a. to try new ideas
   b. to test kites
   c. to stay in the air for one hour

3. Where did the brothers test their gliders and plane? _____

4. How long did their first motor-powered flight last? _____

5. How did the brothers learn about what makes planes work? _____

_____

Diphthong au

Complete each sentence with a word from the word list.
Write the word and circle the **au** diphthong.

Word List

applause	vault	naughty
because	fault	caught

1. The _____ was coming from the theater.

2. The bank teller got money from the _____.

3. We _____ 10 fish on our fishing trip.

4. It was my _____ that we were late for the movie.

5. The _____ puppy chewed up the shoe.

6. We did not have school yesterday _____ it was a holiday.

Multiplication Facts for 7

Multiply to solve the problems.

A. $\begin{array}{r} 3 \\ \times\ 7 \\ \hline \end{array}$

B. $\begin{array}{r} 1 \\ \times\ 7 \\ \hline \end{array}$

C. $\begin{array}{r} 7 \\ \times\ 7 \\ \hline \end{array}$

D. $8 \times 7 = $ _____

E. $7 \times 9 = $ _____

F. $2 \times 7 = $ _____

G. $\begin{array}{r} 7 \\ \times\ 6 \\ \hline \end{array}$

H. $\begin{array}{r} 7 \\ \times\ 4 \\ \hline \end{array}$

I. $\begin{array}{r} 7 \\ \times\ 5 \\ \hline \end{array}$

J. $4 \times 7 = $ _____

K. $7 \times 3 = $ _____

L. $9 \times 7 = $ _____

Multiplication Facts for 8

Multiply to solve the problems.

A. 4
x 8

B. 8
x 8

C. 6
x 8

D. 7 x 8 = _____

E. 3 x 8 = _____

F. 5 x 8 = _____

G. 8
x 0

H. 8
x 1

I. 9
x 8

Diphthong aw

Read each sentence. Write the correct word to complete the sentence.

1. We cut down the tree with a _____.
   (saw   sau)

2. The farmer put _____ in the barn to keep the horses warm.
   (straw   strau)

3. We stood under the _____ so we would not get wet.
   (awning   auning)

4. The little _____ could hardly walk.
   (faun   fawn)

5. Put the meat on the counter to _____.
   (thaw   thau)

6. We gazed in _____ as the acrobat walked on the high wire.
   (aue   awe)

7. My baby brother will _____ before he learns to walk.
   (craul   crawl)

Grid Coordinates

Look at the lines on the grid below. **Grid coordinates** are formed by the letters on the bottom and the numbers on the left side. If you look at the coordinates (C, 4), you should find the Enchanted Woods.

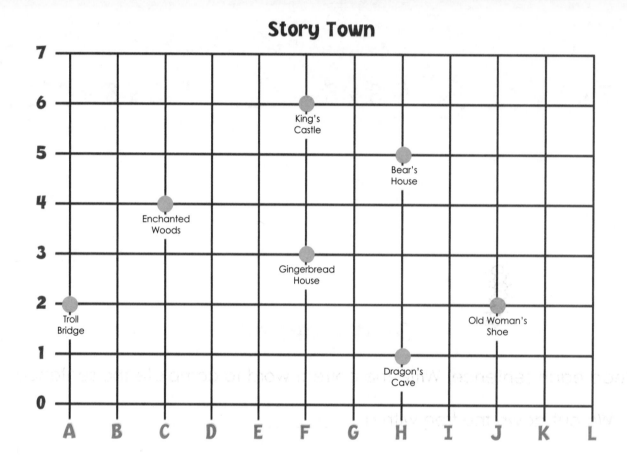

Story Town

Look at each fairy-tale place on the map and find its coordinates.
Write the coordinates for each place beside its name.

King's Castle _____ , _____   **Gingerbread House** _____ , _____

Troll Bridge _____ , _____   **Dragon's Cave** _____ , _____

Bear's House _____ , _____   **Old Woman's Shoe** _____ , _____

Poetry—Haiku

Haiku is a form of Japanese poetry that follows a special pattern of 17 syllables. There are 5 syllables in the first line, 7 in the second line, and 5 in the third line. Most haiku poetry is about nature.

Read the following haiku poem.

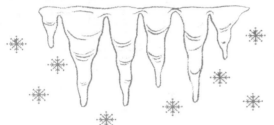

Flakes of snow outside.

Icicles hanging from eaves.

Winter is here now.

Use the lines to write a Haiku poem of your own about apples, summer, or anything you want.

_____

_____

_____

Comparing Fractions

Write >, <, or = in the circle to make a true math statement.

A.
$$\frac{2}{3} \bigcirc \frac{1}{3}$$

B.
$$\frac{12}{13} \bigcirc \frac{11}{13}$$

C.
$$\frac{1}{12} \bigcirc \frac{1}{3}$$

D.
$$\frac{5}{9} \bigcirc \frac{6}{9}$$

E.
$$\frac{2}{6} \bigcirc \frac{3}{6}$$

F.
$$\frac{2}{5} \bigcirc \frac{4}{10}$$

G.
$$\frac{1}{4} \bigcirc \frac{2}{8}$$

H.
$$\frac{3}{4} \bigcirc \frac{1}{4}$$

I.
$$\frac{3}{8} \bigcirc \frac{5}{8}$$

Multiplication Facts for 9

Write the correct factor to complete each multiplication fact.

A. ☐ x 9 = 36

B. 3 x ☐ = 27

C. ☐ x 9 = 18

D.
```
   ☐
 x  9
 ----
  54
```

E.
```
   5
 x ☐
 ----
  45
```

F.
```
   ☐
 x  9
 ----
  63
```

G. 1 x ☐ = 9

H. 2 x ☐ = 18

I. ☐ x 9 = 0

J. ☐ x 7 = 63

K. 9 x ☐ = 9

L. 9 x ☐ = 45

Alphabetical Order

Number the words in each group alphabetically from 1 to 5.
You will need to look all the way to the fourth or fifth letter in
each group before you start numbering.

1. _____ peanut
_____ peacock
_____ pear
_____ peak
_____ peat

2. _____ greet
_____ greenhouse
_____ grew
_____ grenade
_____ gremlin

3. _____ alligator
_____ alley
_____ allow
_____ allude
_____ allspice

4. _____ iceberg
_____ icehouse
_____ icebox
_____ Iceland
_____ icebreaker

Singular and Plural Possessives

Put an apostrophe in the correct position. Then, complete the sentence.

1. Several astronauts spacesuits _____ .

2. That boys football _____ .

3. The three poodles fur_____ .

4. The four cats claws_____ .

5. This weeks laundry basket _____ .

6. My three friends bikes _____ .

7. The suns rays _____ .

8. This robins nest _____ .

9. The elfs voice_____ .

10. The two beavers dams _____ .

Using Context Clues

When you come to a word you don't know, use the **context clues**, or other words around it, to help you figure out the meaning.

Use context clues to figure out the meaning of each highlighted word below. Circle the correct meaning.

1. The green light coming from the haunted house was frightening. It was an **eerie** sight!

    a. green   b. spooky   c. funny

2. We must leave soon. We must **depart** as soon as everyone is ready.

    a. watch   b. leave   c. sign

3. The **clasp** of the seat belt was not fastened correctly.

    a. buckle   b. strap   c. seat

Using Prefixes

A **prefix** is a syllable or syllables placed at the beginning of a base word to change its meaning. Here are some examples of prefixes:

un = not   **re** = again   **dis** = apart from, not

For each sentence, write a prefix that can be added to the highlighted word. Write the new word and its meaning.

1. I am **able** to do all of my work.

   prefix: _____   new word: _____

   meaning: _____

2. Mother will **agree** that my allowance should be more if I rake leaves.

   prefix: _____   new word: _____

   meaning: _____

Alphabetical Order

Number the names in each group alphabetically from 1 to 5.
Remember to alphabetize names by the **last** name.
Do you recognize any of these authors?

A. _____ Lewis Carroll

_____ Louisa May Alcott

_____ Mark Twain

_____ Hans Christian Andersen

_____ Charles Dickens

B. _____ Jules Verne

_____ Edgar Allan Poe

_____ J. R. R. Tolkien

_____ Robert Louis Stevenson

_____ Sir James Barrie

Working with Money

Read each problem and circle the correct answer.
Use extra paper to help you solve the problems if needed.

A. Jarvis has 5 quarters, 10 dimes, 3 nickels, and 37 pennies. How much money does he have?

$2.50 $2.67 $2.77 $3.77

B. Michael has $6.25. If he rents a video game for $4.75, how much change will he have?

$2.50 $2.75 $1.25 $1.50

C. Michelle wants to purchase an $11.00 baseball cap, a $15.00 shirt, and a $1.00 pack of gum. She has a $50.00 bill. How much change will she receive?

$27.00 $23.00 $77.00 $50.00

Diphthong ew

Use a word from the word list to complete each sentence correctly.

Word List	knew	threw	flew	review	
	chew	blew	view		newspaper

1. Be sure to _____ the last five chapters before the test.

2. Juan _____ the ball across the playground to Tony.

3. The _____ of the trees from the mountaintop was amazing.

4. I _____ Susan would like the birthday gift you bought for her.

5. The _____ is on the kitchen table.

6. Use your teeth to _____ your food.

7. I watched the bird as it _____ away.

8. The wind _____ the papers across the street.

Entry Words and Guide Words

Entry words are listed in the dictionary.
Guide words are words at the top of each page in the dictionary.

Look at each entry word and the guide words beside it. Decide if the entry word would come between the two guide words alphabetically in a dictionary. Write **yes** or **no** on the line.

	Entry Word	Guide Word	
1.	pyramid	puzzle, python	_____
2.	acrobat	acme, action	_____
3.	tutor	twinge, type	_____
4.	wrist	worsen, wrestle	_____
5.	blob	bleach, block	_____
6.	hummingbird	hunch, husky	_____
7.	crimson	crime, crocodile	_____
8.	fill	file, film	_____
9.	injure	inherit, ink	_____
10.	silver	silly, single	_____

Look at the guide words at the top of each word list below.
Circle only the words that would be entry words on a
dictionary page with those guide words.

A. lead–lease	B. crocus–crossing	C. gift–globe	D. rude–rummy
lean	cricket	giant	royal
leap	crop	give	ruler
left	croquet	glove	ruin
leaf	cross	glass	ruby

Review Multiplication Facts 6-9

Complete the multiplication facts. Do you see any patterns?

A. 6 x 0 = _____   7 x 0 = _____   8 x 0 = _____   9 x 0 = _____

B. 6 x 1 = _____   7 x 1 = _____   8 x 1 = _____   9 x 1 = _____

C. 6 x 2 = _____   7 x 2 = _____   8 x 2 = _____   9 x 2 = _____

D. 6 x 3 = _____   7 x 3 = _____   8 x 3 = _____   9 x 3 = _____

E. 6 x 4 = _____   7 x 4 = _____   8 x 4 = _____   9 x 4 = _____

F. 6 x 5 = _____   7 x 5 = _____   8 x 5 = _____   9 x 5 = _____

Diphthong oi

Use an **oi** word from the word list to complete each sentence.

Word List

voice
point
join
doily
soil
appoint
joint
boil
coin

1. My mother put a lace _____ on the table.

2. The elbow is a _____ in the arm.

3. The students had to _____ a class president.

4. Plant the seed in the _____.

5. I want to _____ the baseball team.

6. The singer had a lovely _____.

7. The change purse had only one _____ in it.

8. The water in the pot got so hot that it began to _____.

9. It is hard to write well with a pencil that has a dull _____.

Diphthong ou

Write each **ou** word from the word list under its rhyming word.
Circle the **ou** diphthong in each word.

scout

mound

Word List

sound
sprout
pout
trout
stout
bound
round
about
surround
shout
pound
hound

_____

_____

_____

_____

_____

_____

_____

_____

_____

_____

_____

_____

Review Multiplication Facts 6-9

Circle the correct product for each multiplication fact.

A. 6 x 7 =
42
12

B. 9 x 6 =
11
54

C. 4 x 6 =
24
16

D. 4 x 7¢ =
28¢
40¢

E. 8 x 8 =
40
64

F. 5 x 9¢ =
18¢
45¢

Definitions

Mary Martin, alias Peter Pan

Mary Martin is **fondly** remembered as the **petite** star who won an Emmy award for her **performance** in the TV production of *Peter Pan*. This cheerful, **exuberant** star was born Mary Virginia Martin on December 1, 1913. When she was 16, she married Benjamin Hagman. They had a son, Larry, who is **renowned** for his roles in the TV series *I Dream of Jeannie* and *Dallas*. Mary **exhibited** a talent for **aerial** ballet. After teaching and performing dance for several years, she **journeyed** to Hollywood to further her **career**. She had many **roles** in films and on Broadway.

Read the paragraph above carefully. Write the letter of the definition on the line next to each numbered word.

1. fondly _____
2. petite _____
3. performance _____
4. exuberant _____
5. renowned _____
6. roles _____
7. exhibited _____
8. aerial _____
9. journeyed _____
10. career _____

a. traveled

b. job, occupation

c. well known, famous

d. lovingly

e. enthusiastic

f. in the air

g. parts or characters played by an actor

h. small, little

i. the act of performing

j. showed or displayed

Constructing Stories

Write five sentences about the picture. Use the boxes at the end of each line to number your sentences in story order. Write your story and give it a title. Be sure to use capital letters and periods.

1. _____ ☐

2. _____ ☐

3. _____ ☐

4. _____ ☐

5. _____ ☐

Things to Think About

Who is this story about? Where does this story take place? How does this story begin? What happens next? How will this story end?

_____

_____

_____

_____

_____

_____

_____

_____

Reading a Table

A **table** is a compact, orderly arrangement of facts or figures, usually presented in rows or columns.

Ross's Movie Rental Review

Use this table to answer the questions below.

	Sun.	Mon.	Tues.	Wed.	Thurs.	Fri.	Sat.
Chuckie Chipmunk	1	4	0	2	3	5	2
Swamp Critters	2	3	1	2	0	2	3
Hero for a Day	0	6	2	1	4	5	5
Scary Vegetables	1	2	2	4	0	3	4
Halloween Howl	1	3	2	0	0	2	2

The numbers tell how many times each movie was rented each day.

1. Which movie was rented the most on Monday? _____
2. Which movie was rented the least on Monday? _____
3. Which movie was not rented on Tuesday? _____
4. Which movie was not rented on Wednesday or Thursday? _____
5. Were more movies rented on Saturday or Sunday? _____
6. Was *Chuckie Chipmunk* rented more than *Halloween Howl*? _____
7. On what day were the fewest movies rented? _____
8. Were more movies rented on Tuesday or Wednesday? _____
9. Which two days had seven movie rentals each? _____
10. How many times was *Swamp Critters* rented this week? _____

Beat the Clock (Multiplication Facts Review)

A.	$9 \times 1 =$ ____	$5 \times 8 =$ ____	$2 \times 5 =$ ____	$7 \times 5 =$ ____	$4 \times 7 =$ ____
B.	$0 \times 5 =$ ____	$8 \times 0 =$ ____	$8 \times 6 =$ ____	$0 \times 9 =$ ____	$6 \times 3 =$ ____
C.	$9 \times 6 =$ ____	$7 \times 4 =$ ____	$7 \times 0 =$ ____	$4 \times 4 =$ ____	$0 \times 3 =$ ____
D.	$6 \times 4 =$ ____	$1 \times 7 =$ ____	$3 \times 7 =$ ____	$3 \times 1 =$ ____	$5 \times 3 =$ ____
E.	$9 \times 9 =$ ____	$9 \times 3 =$ ____	$0 \times 4 =$ ____	$7 \times 9 =$ ____	$6 \times 0 =$ ____
F.	$1 \times 3 =$ ____	$4 \times 8 =$ ____	$5 \times 7 =$ ____	$5 \times 2 =$ ____	$2 \times 1 =$ ____
G.	$9 \times 4 =$ ____	$1 \times 0 =$ ____	$7 \times 1 =$ ____	$0 \times 0 =$ ____	$3 \times 6 =$ ____
H.	$4 \times 3 =$ ____	$7 \times 8 =$ ____	$2 \times 4 =$ ____	$8 \times 5 =$ ____	$1 \times 2 =$ ____
I.	$3 \times 8 =$ ____	$9 \times 8 =$ ____	$5 \times 1 =$ ____	$3 \times 0 =$ ____	$7 \times 3 =$ ____
J.	$8 \times 1 =$ ____	$5 \times 6 =$ ____	$2 \times 0 =$ ____	$6 \times 2 =$ ____	$0 \times 8 =$ ____
K.	$9 \times 7 =$ ____	$0 \times 1 =$ ____	$6 \times 6 =$ ____	$1 \times 6 =$ ____	$2 \times 9 =$ ____
L.	$5 \times 0 =$ ____	$6 \times 9 =$ ____	$3 \times 2 =$ ____	$8 \times 0 =$ ____	$4 \times 0 =$ ____
M.	$7 \times 2 =$ ____	$2 \times 6 =$ ____	$0 \times 7 =$ ____	$3 \times 5 =$ ____	$4 \times 6 =$ ____
N.	$2 \times 3 =$ ____	$5 \times 9 =$ ____	$4 \times 2 =$ ____	$1 \times 1 =$ ____	$7 \times 7 =$ ____
O.	$6 \times 5 =$ ____	$0 \times 6 =$ ____	$5 \times 5 =$ ____	$9 \times 2 =$ ____	$8 \times 2 =$ ____
P.	$3 \times 9 =$ ____	$6 \times 1 =$ ____	$1 \times 5 =$ ____	$2 \times 8 =$ ____	$2 \times 2 =$ ____
Q.	$1 \times 4 =$ ____	$1 \times 9 =$ ____	$4 \times 9 =$ ____	$0 \times 2 =$ ____	$6 \times 7 =$ ____
R.	$8 \times 4 =$ ____	$4 \times 5 =$ ____	$7 \times 6 =$ ____	$9 \times 5 =$ ____	$5 \times 4 =$ ____
S.	$8 \times 8 =$ ____	$6 \times 8 =$ ____	$9 \times 0 =$ ____	$3 \times 3 =$ ____	$8 \times 7 =$ ____
T.	$3 \times 4 =$ ____	$4 \times 1 =$ ____	$2 \times 7 =$ ____	$8 \times 3 =$ ____	$1 \times 8 =$ ____

Time: [ ]   **Number correct:** [ ]

Secret Codes and Puzzles

1

Use the secret code to solve the riddle.

What would your nose be if it were 12 inches long?

✻ ☞ ☞ ✚   ◆

Secret Code Key

◆ = A	☀ = G	✠ = L	✱ = Q	◆ = V
✧ = B	✴ = H	☎ = M	✳ = R	✻ = W
★ = C	✣ = I	✿ = N	✜ = S	☐ = X
✪ = D	✦ = J	☞ = O	✲ = T	● = Y
✩ = E	✚ = K	✈ = P	✹ = U	☼ = Z
✚ = F				

3

Use the secret code to solve the riddle.

What kind of house is the easiest to lift?

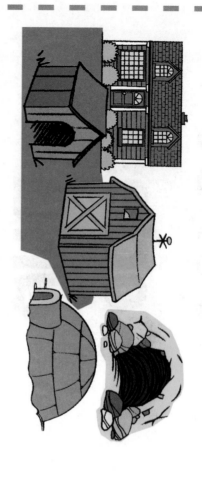

3	23	4	10	22	13	22	18	17	5	12

Secret Code Key

3 = A	10 = G	23 = L	6 = Q	14 = V
7 = B	22 = H	20 = M	21 = R	2 = W
11 = C	4 = I	25 = N	5 = S	26 = X
1 = D	16 = J	18 = O	13 = T	14 = Y
12 = E	9 = K	24 = P	17 = U	8 = Z
15 = F				

2

Farmer Potter's cornfield is full of hungry crows. Find out if there are enough ears of corn on the page for each crow to have two ears. Circle the correct sentence below the picture.

There is enough corn for each crow to have two ears.

There is not enough corn for each crow to have two ears.

4

74

Use the secret code to solve the riddle.

What's worse than a giraffe with a sore throat?

$$\overline{35}\ \overline{15}\ \overline{30}\ \overline{5}\ \overline{125}\ \overline{10}\ \overline{115}\ \overline{30}\ \overline{70}\ \overline{30}$$

$$\overline{50}\ \overline{10}\ \overline{125}\ \overline{45}\ \overline{105}\ \overline{80}\ \overline{60}\ \overline{30}$$

$$\overline{85}\ \overline{30}\ \overline{30}\ \overline{125}\ !$$

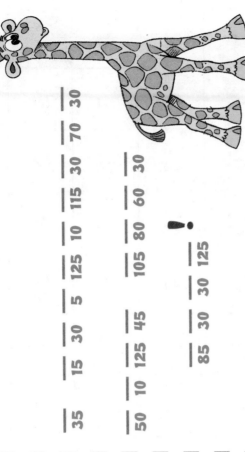

Secret Code Key

35 = A	100 = Q	130 = V
55 = B	110 = G	120 = L	100 = Q	50 = W
15 = C	45 = H	95 = M	60 = R	65 = X
70 = D	10 = I	5 = N	105 = S
30 = E	75 = J	80 = O	125 = T	90 = Y
85 = F	40 = K	115 = P	20 = U	25 = Z

5

Help the hiker get back to his camp. Color the stones with multiples of 5. A path will appear to lead the hiker to his camp. The first and last stones are already marked.

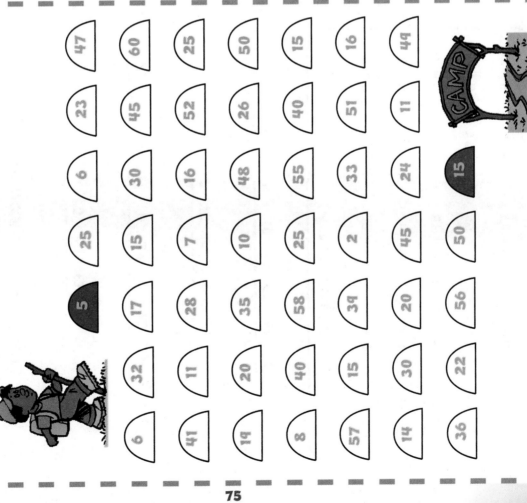

6	32	**5**	25	6	23	47
41	11	17	15	30	45	60
14	20	28	7	16	52	25
8	40	35	10	48	26	50
57	15	58	25	55	40	15
14	30	39	2	33	51	16
36	22	56	50	45	24	11
			15			49

CAMP

7

75

Color a path across and down to move from start to finish. Each new square in the path must have a number greater than the previous number in the path. The first and last squares are already marked.

1	5	3	4	22	15	4
0	9	12	7	30	10	22
2	6	13	10	9	7	3
9	4	16	20	11	4	9
33	8	14	24	21	17	2
21	24	19	27	29	25	15
6	30	2	18	30	35	33
15	18	4	12	27	42	50

Use the secret code to solve the riddle.

What is yellow, weighs 1,000 pounds, and sings?

___ ___ ___
3   69   45

___ ___ ___ ___   —   ___ ___ ___ ___ ___ ___ ___
27 54 75 51   9   24 57 42 66 51 42

___ ___ ___ ___ ___
72 45 24 57 42

___ ___ ___ ___ ___ ___ ___ ___
18 30 57 30 66 54 51 36

Secret Code Key

30 = A	15 = G	33 = L	39 = Q	75 = V
21 = B	9 = H	6 = M	66 = R	69 = W
18 = C	6 = M	57 = N	36 = S	48 = X
42 = D	54 = I	45 = O	3 = T	12 = Y
51 = E	78 = J	45 = O	3 = T	12 = Y
27 = F	60 = K	72 = P	24 = U	63 = Z

Multiplication Facts 0–9 Review

Problem List

9 x 1 = __9__

8 x 5 = ___	5 x 8 = ___
7 x 5 = ___	9 x 9 = ___
9 x 3 = ___	3 x 8 = ___
7 x 7 = ___	4 x 9 = ___
6 x 6 = ___	3 x 6 = ___
7 x 4 = ___	0 x 8 = ___
8 x 4 = ___	9 x 4 = ___
9 x 2 = ___	9 x 5 = ___
8 x 8 = ___	9 x 7 = ___

Multiply to solve the problems in the problem list. Then, find the same problems in the puzzle. Circle the hidden problems and write **x** and **=** in the correct places. Problems are hidden across and down.

0	9 x 1 = 9	18	11	16	72	8	5	40
8	28	5	45	37	7	6	81	1	8	7
0	24	6	6	36	0	8	0	33	4	10
7	12	0	9	3	27	63	14	20	32	2
9	2	18	25	6	11	81	0	3	5	8
16	48	9	11	4	9	36	18	8	55
3	12	5	22	21	54	30	9	40	0
6	1	45	15	7	60	20	7	35	21
18	7	5	35	7	23	0	63	35	2
7	4	8	9	25	3	12	9	9	81
4	26	8	25	7	7	49	7	2	3
21	28	5	64	36	3	1	22	5	17	18
3	9	36	6	3	20	8	40	24	9	13
4	2	3	8	24	3	4	3	17	4	8
13	36	6	4	20	6	1	8	5	36	3
5	7	9	16	4	18	10	13	8	9	11

Compare and Contrast

Fill in the blanks with words that tell how a tree and flower are alike and different. The first ones have been done for you.

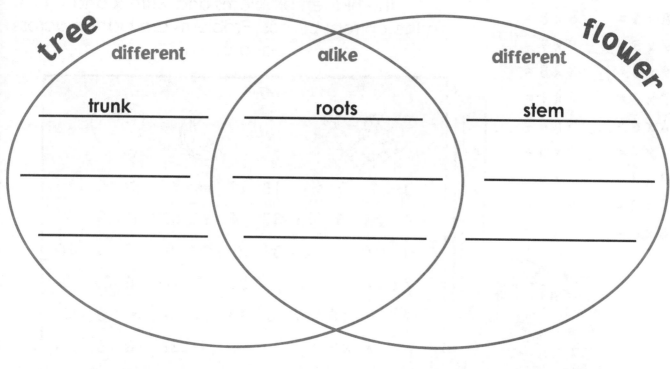

Write two paragraphs below. In the first paragraph, tell how trees and flowers are alike. Tell how each is different in the second paragraph. Give each paragraph a title.

Multiplying One- and Two-Digit Numbers

Rule:

Multiply ones, then regroup.
Multiply tens, then add extra tens.

Example:

23	23
x 6	x 6
8	138

Solve each problem. Write the answer in the space provided.

A. 10
  x 5

B. 10
  x 3

C. 12
  x 2

D. 15
  x 4

E. 19
  x 2

F. 31
  x 4

G. 62
  x 2

H. 27
  x 3

I. 54
  x 3

J. 79
  x 3

K. 87
  x 5

L. 90
  x 4

Diphthong ow

Write each word from the word list beside its rhyming word.
Circle the **ow** diphthong in each word on the line.

Word List

brow

powder

scowl

town

tower

prowl _____ _____

power _____ _____

bow _____ _____

down _____ _____

powder _____ _____

BONUS

Write another word with an **ow** diphthong to
rhyme with each word in the above activity.

Drawing Conclusions

Read the story. Then, answer the questions.

Photograph

Jack was not comfortable. His new shirt was too stiff and his tie felt tight. Mother had fussed over his hair trying to get it to look just right. She made him scrub his hands three times to get the dirt from under his fingernails! Finally, his mom said he was ready. She smiled and said that Jack looked very handsome. Jack frowned, but knew he could not tell his mom how he felt. This was important to her. Jack sat on a special stool that turned and looked at the camera. He didn't feel like smiling, but he did his best. "Perfect!" said the man behind the camera as he snapped the shot. Jack posed two more times, and then the man said they were finished. The first thing Jack did was take off his tie!

1. What was Jack doing?

_____

2. What clues tell you where Jack is?

_____

3. How does Jack feel about this?

_____

4. What clues tell you how Jack feels?

_____

5. Who was the man that said "perfect"?

_____

6. Why did Jack take off his tie?

_____

Counting Syllables

Syllables represent the number of vowel sounds heard in words.

Examples: what – 1 vowel sound and 1 syllable
pencil – 2 vowel sounds and 2 syllables
animal – 3 vowel sounds and 3 syllables

Read each word below. Use the line to write the number of syllables in the word. Listen to make sure that the number of vowel sounds equals the number of syllables for each word.

1. apple _____
2. prune _____
3. cherry _____

4. banana _____
5. lemon _____
6. pear _____

7. watermelon _____
8. plum _____
9. strawberry _____

Alphabetical Order

To alphabetize titles you need to put small words like **A**, **The**, or **An** at the end of a title.

Example: The Cat in the Hat would be Cat in the Hat, The.

Number the titles from 1 to 9 as they should appear alphabetically.

_____ *Charlotte's Friend*
_____ *Amos Goes Camping*
_____ *The Chocolate Prize*
_____ *Harvey's Mystery*
_____ *The Whale Watchers*
_____ *A Lion and a Bear*
_____ *Where the River Ends*
_____ *Cats for Sale*
_____ *The Needlefish Return*

Multiplying One- and Three-Digit Numbers

Rule:

1. Multiply ones, then regroup.
2. Multiply tens, then add extra tens.
3. Multiply hundreds.
4. Regroup as needed.

Example:

$$\begin{array}{r} \overset{1}{4}53 \\ \times\ \ 4 \\ \hline 2 \end{array} \quad \begin{array}{r} \overset{1}{4}53 \\ \times\ \ 4 \\ \hline 12 \end{array} \quad \begin{array}{r} \overset{2}{4}\overset{1}{5}3 \\ \times\ \ 4 \\ \hline 1{,}812 \end{array}$$

Solve the problems. Write the answers in the space provided.

A.
$$\begin{array}{r} 100 \\ \times\ \ 3 \\ \hline \end{array}$$

B.
$$\begin{array}{r} 120 \\ \times\ \ 2 \\ \hline \end{array}$$

C.
$$\begin{array}{r} 278 \\ \times\ \ 4 \\ \hline \end{array}$$

D.
$$\begin{array}{r} 329 \\ \times\ \ 3 \\ \hline \end{array}$$

E.
$$\begin{array}{r} 422 \\ \times\ \ 5 \\ \hline \end{array}$$

F.
$$\begin{array}{r} 705 \\ \times\ \ 4 \\ \hline \end{array}$$

G.
$$\begin{array}{r} 827 \\ \times\ \ 9 \\ \hline \end{array}$$

H.
$$\begin{array}{r} 926 \\ \times\ \ 7 \\ \hline \end{array}$$

Understanding What I Read

What Eats the Firefly?

There are very few animals that are not eaten by something. No creature, however, eats the firefly, or lightning bug. The adult firefly has almost no predators. Birds, insect-eating mammals, reptiles, and fish do not eat them. Sharks are also bothered by them. They will swish around wildly and then seem to be paralyzed with fear when fireflies are put in their tank.

Read the paragraph. Then, answer the questions.

1. What is the main idea of the paragraph?_____

2. What is another name for a firefly? _____

3. Describe what the fearless shark will do if a firefly is in its tank. _____

_____

4. What do you think a predator is?_____

Reading a Bar Graph

This bar graph shows the different eye colors of the children in three third grade classes.

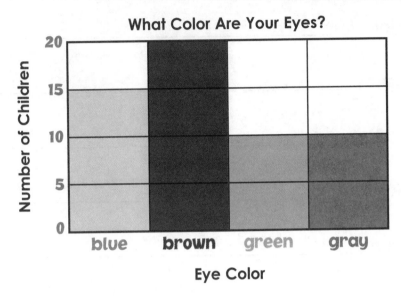

What Color Are Your Eyes?

Look at the graph and answer the following questions.

A. How many children have green eyes? _____

B. How many more children have blue eyes than gray eyes? _____

C. How many more children have brown eyes than blue eyes? _____

D. This graph lists eye color for how many third graders? _____

E. Which two eye colors are found in an equal number of students?

_____

F. Make one statement about this graph based on the data given.

_____

Diphthong oy

Look at the highlighted letters in each pair of words. Circle the word that is spelled correctly, and then use the word in a sentence.

1. enjoy   enjoi   _____

2. destroi   destroy   _____

3. loial   loyal   _____

4. royal   roial   _____

5. annoy   annoi   _____

6. toi   toy   _____

Multiplying Two- and Three-Digit Numbers

Rule:

1. **Multiply ones by ones, tens, and hundreds. Regroup as needed.**

2. **Multiply tens by ones, tens, and hundreds. Regroup as needed.**

3. **Add the two numbers to find the final product.**

Example:

$$
\begin{array}{r}
325 \\
\times\ 43 \\
\hline
975
\end{array}
\qquad
\begin{array}{r}
325 \\
\times\ 43 \\
\hline
975 \\
13000
\end{array}
\qquad
\begin{array}{r}
325 \\
\times\ 43 \\
\hline
975 \\
+13000 \\
\hline
13{,}975
\end{array}
$$

Solve the problems.

A. $\begin{array}{r} 203 \\ \times\ 12 \\ \hline \end{array}$ B. $\begin{array}{r} 330 \\ \times\ 25 \\ \hline \end{array}$ C. $\begin{array}{r} 633 \\ \times\ 61 \\ \hline \end{array}$ D. $\begin{array}{r} 567 \\ \times\ 38 \\ \hline \end{array}$

Multiplication Rounding and Estimating

Rule:
Since it is easier to multiply by numbers ending in 0, it can be useful to estimate an approximate answer by rounding.

Example:
26 x 9 = ___
26 rounds up to **30**,
so the estimated product is:
30 x 9 = 270

Round the two-digit factor to the nearest ten.
Multiply to find the estimated product.

A.   18
   x 2

B.   23
   x 5

C.   15
   x 3

D.   24
   x 9

E.   58
   x 5

F.   64
   x 7

G.   75
   x 4

H.   81
   x 8

Adjectives

Use the line in front of each noun to
write an **adjective** that describes the noun.

1. _____ rain

2. _____ table

3. _____ flower

4. _____ day

5. _____ fruit

5. _____ petal

7. _____ grass

8. _____ friend

9. _____ lake

10. _____ house

Prefixes and Suffixes

Base Words	**Prefixes**	**Suffixes**
are the root words that are used to make other words.	are letters that are put in **front** of base words to change the meaning of the base words.	are letters added to the **end** of base words to change the meaning of the base word.
helpful	**re**write	health**y**
The root word is **help**.	The prefix **re** changes the meaning of the base word **write**.	The suffix **y** changes the meaning of the base word **health**.

For each question below, decide which part of the word is highlighted in blue. Write **base word**, **prefix**, or **suffix** on the line.

1. punish**ment** _____

2. **dark**ness _____

3. dis**appear** _____

4. pre**cook** _____

5. **pre**soak _____

6. **proud**ly _____

7. **place**ment _____

8. dis**trust** _____

9. **color**less _____

10. friend**ly** _____

11. sick**ness** _____

12. sugar**less** _____

13. **fool**ish _____

14. **brown**ish _____

15. re**fill** _____

16. **re**pay _____

17. un**sure** _____

18. lone**ly** _____

Capitalization

In the story below, circle each letter that should be a capital letter.
Add an ending to the story.

my birthday

today is my birthday. i am nine years old. i was born on wednesday, april 12, in billings, montana. my family will celebrate my birthday tonight. mom will cook her special spaghetti dinner just for me. dad will be home from work early. my brother, david, and my sister, rose, will be here, too. after dinner grandma and grandpa will come. we will all eat cake and ice cream. they will sing "happy birthday" to me. then, i . . .

_____

_____

_____

_____

_____

_____

_____

_____

_____

Fact and Opinion

A **fact** is something that is real and could happen.

An **opinion** is something that is believed to be true but may not be.

There are apples on the tree.

Those apples are beautiful.

Mark each sentence with an **F** for fact or an **O** for opinion.

_____ 1. My mother fixes dinner every night at 6:00.

_____ 2. Chocolate pie is the best dessert.

_____ 3. The state of Wisconsin is a part of the United States.

_____ 4. People can go to a movie theater to watch movies.

_____ 5. It is more fun to rent a movie and watch it at home than to go to a theater.

Problem Solving with Multiplication

Solve the word problems. Show your work and write the answers in the space provided.

A. Sophia's Bakery sold 8 cakes each day for 21 days. How many cakes did the bakery sell in all?

B. Regina made 49 gift baskets each week for 5 weeks. Estimate how many gift baskets she made.

C. For 21 days of camp, Melanie collected 2 souvenirs each day. How many souvenirs did she collect in all?

D. Donna sold 136 bags of popcorn at the movie theater for 24 days. Estimate to find out about how many bags of popcorn Donna sold.

Classification

The words below all have something in common. What heading can you give the list that will name all the words? Write a heading on the line **Main Heading**. Sort the words in the box into two categories. Write the words on the lines. Write a subheading for each group.

big	bitty	enormous	fat	giant	gigantic
great	huge	large	little	long	mammoth
miniature	petite	short	skinny	slight	small
tall	teeny	thin	tiny	vast	wee

_____
Main Heading

_____   _____
Subheading   **Subheading**

Telling Time

Read each problem and circle the correct answer for each.

A. Which clock shows 8:30?

B. Which clock has the same time as the first one?

C. Which clock shows 15 minutes before 7?

D. **Quarter past four** is another way of saying which of the following times?

Beginning Digraphs: ch, sh, th

Say the name of each picture. Circle the beginning digraph.

1.		2.		3.		4.	
	ch		ch		ch		ch
	th		th		th		th
	sh		sh		sh		sh

Say the name of each picture. Write the beginning digraph **ch**, **sh**, or **th** to complete the word.

5.

_____urch

6.

_____icken

7.

_____ell

8.

_____imble

Beginning Digraph ph

Read the words. Underline the beginning digraph **ph** in each word.

1. physical
2. pharmacy
3. photograph

4. pharaoh
5. phantom
6. phonograph

7. physician
8. photosynthesis
9. phonics

Read the words. Circle each word that begins with the digraph **ph**.
Place an **x** on any word that does not begin with this digraph.

10. phony
11. photography
12. pinch
13. poetry

14. page
15. phobia
16. puddle
17. pharmacist

18. phase
19. please
20. piano
21. paper

Elapsed Time

Find each time. All times are A.M. Write the answer on the line provided.

A. 30 minutes after

_____

B. 15 minutes after

_____

C. 15 minutes after

_____

D. 30 minutes after

_____

E. 30 minutes before

_____

F. 1 hour before

_____

Reading a Calendar

Mrs. Simms has two children, Jay and Joy. The calendar shows
Jay's baseball games and Joy's soccer games in April.
Use the calendar to answer the questions.

April

Sunday	Monday	Tuesday	Wednesday	Thursday	Friday	Saturday
		1 Jay's game	2	3 Joy's game	4	5 Jay's & Joy's games
6	7 Jay's game	8 Joy's game	9	10 Joy's game	11	12 Joy's game
13 Jay's game	14	15 Jay's game	16	17 Joy's game	18	19 Jay's & Joy's games
20	21	22 Jay's game	23	24 Joy's game	25 Joy's game	26 Jay's game
27	28	29 Jay's game	30			

1. Who plays the first game of the month?

   _____

2. What day of the week is the first game?

   _____

3. Who has more games, Jay or Joy?

   _____

4. Who has a game on the second Tuesday of the month?

   _____

5. On April 24, Joy has a game. What day of the week is that?

   _____

6. How many games does Joy play on Tuesdays and Saturdays?

   _____

7. On which dates do both Jay and Joy have games?

   _____

8. A week begins on Sunday and ends on Saturday. In which week are the most games played?

   _____

9. Are there any days of the week in which no games are played?

   _____

Descriptive Writing

Read the following paragraph.

I have a favorite pair of shoes. They are old. My mom doesn't like them. She wants me to throw them away and get a new pair. I would rather keep my old shoes.

Now, read the same paragraph with adjectives and more description added.

I have a favorite pair of shoes. They are old and comfortable. The shoes are blue. The left shoe has a hole in the toe, and the right has a broken shoelace. Both of them have holes worn in the bottom. My mom doesn't like my old shoes. They are very dirty. She wants me to throw them away and get a new pair. I would rather keep my old, comfortable shoes.

Read the following paragraph. Then, rewrite it to make it more interesting using adjectives and more description.

Yesterday my family took a train ride. There were passenger cars, boxcars, and an engine. A caboose was at the end. The whistle blew. We were off! Smoke blew from the engine. The cars began to rock. I would like to ride on a train again.

_____

_____

_____

_____

_____

_____

_____

Division Facts 0-1

Rules: 0 divided by any number will always equal 0.

Any number divided by 1 will always equal that number.

Examples: $0 \div 5 = 0$ $8 \div 1 = 8$

Solve each problem. Write the answer on the line.

A. $0 \div 12 =$ _____   **B.** $0 \div 10 =$ _____   **C.** $3 \div 1 =$ _____

D. $5 \div 1 =$ _____   **E.** $0 \div 3 =$ _____   **F.** $0 \div 6 =$ _____

G. $4 \div 1 =$ _____   **H.** $0 \div 9 =$ _____   **I.** $0 \div 1 =$ _____

J. $11 \div 1 =$ _____   **K.** $7 \div 1 =$ _____   **L.** $0 \div 2 =$ _____

M. $9 \div 1 =$ _____   **N.** $1 \div 1 =$ _____   **O.** $0 \div 8 =$ _____

Beginning Digraph qu

Say the name of each picture. Circle the picture if the word begins with the digraph **qu**. Put an **x** on the picture if the word does not begin with **qu**.

1.    2.    3.    4.

Read each word. If the word begins with the digraph **qu**,
write **qu** on the line. If not, leave the line blank.

5. quarrel _____   **6.** quest _____   **7.** shadow _____

8. suntan _____   **9.** quiet _____   **10.** frown _____

11. quack _____   **12.** powder _____   **13.** quality _____

Prefixes and Suffixes

Divide the words below by separating the prefixes, suffixes, and base words.

Note: Sometimes the silent **e** is removed from the base word when a suffix is added. **Example:** remove – removable.
Add the silent **e** to the base words that need it.

	Prefix	Base Word	Suffix
1. refreshment	re	fresh	ment
2. undependable			
3. enlargement			
4. unbelievable			
5. disappointment			
6. untruthful			
7. prearrangement			

Division Facts 2–4

Rule:

10 items placed in groups of two equal 5 groups.

Example:

 =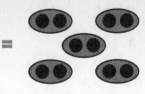

Solve each problem. Write the answer on the line.

A. $16 \div 2 =$ _____   **B.** $8 \div 2 =$ _____   **C.** $4 \div 4 =$ _____

D. $14 \div 2 =$ _____   **E.** $24 \div 2 =$ _____   **F.** $48 \div 4 =$ _____

G. $12 \div 4 =$ _____   **H.** $36 \div 3 =$ _____   **I.** $36 \div 4 =$ _____

J. $22 \div 2 =$ _____   **K.** $18 \div 2 =$ _____   **L.** $20 \div 2 =$ _____

M. $20 \div 4 =$ _____   **N.** $15 \div 3 =$ _____   **O.** $2 \div 2 =$ _____

P. $28 \div 4 =$ _____   **Q.** $33 \div 3 =$ _____   **R.** $24 \div 3 =$ _____

Division Facts 1–5

Divide to solve the problems in the problem list. Then, find the same problems in the puzzle. Circle each hidden problem and write ÷ and = in the correct places. Problems are hidden across and down.

Problem List

6 ÷ 2 = __3__

4 ÷ 2 = ____

3 ÷ 3 = ____

15 ÷ 5 = ____

20 ÷ 5 = ____

25 ÷ 5 = ____

10 ÷ 2 = ____

8 ÷ 4 = ____

9 ÷ 3 = ____

20 ÷ 4 = ____

15 ÷ 3 = ____

12 ÷ 3 = ____

12 ÷ 4 = ____

5 ÷ 5 = ____

10 ÷ 5 = ____

8 ÷ 2 = ____

6 ÷ 3 = ____

16 ÷ 4 = ____

1	8	2	4	15	8	12	4	2	2	3
6	1	3	4	10	20	4	5	6	0	7
12	12	4	12	5	1	1	2	÷ 2	5	2
3	3	16	4	2	16	15	6	= 3	8	6
6	4	1	3	1	4	3	9	3	3	5
3	8	4	2	3	4	5	1	8	0	5
2	1	15	3	7	20	2	20	5	4	1
7	16	5	2	25	5	5	3	1	20	3
11	6	3	4	7	9	2	5	5	9	4
8	1	5	1	10	2	5	3	3	1	8
10	7	12	3	10	4	8	1	2	3	3
3	6	2	5	2	1	6	25	1	6	2

Division Facts 5–7

Solve each problem. Then, write the answer on the line provided.

A. 30 ÷ 5 = _____   54 ÷ 6 = _____   49 ÷ 7 = _____

B. 12 ÷ 6 = _____   15 ÷ 5 = _____   60 ÷ 6 = _____

C. 40 ÷ 5 = _____   28 ÷ 7 = _____   25 ÷ 5 = _____

D. 18 ÷ 6 = _____   70 ÷ 7 = _____   60 ÷ 5 = _____

E. 42 ÷ 6 = _____   63 ÷ 7 = _____   77 ÷ 7 = _____

F. 35 ÷ 7 = _____   7 ÷ 7 = _____   14 ÷ 7 = _____

G. 48 ÷ 6 = _____   36 ÷ 6 = _____   10 ÷ 5 = _____

H. 20 ÷ 5 = _____   55 ÷ 5 = _____   84 ÷ 7 = _____

I. 56 ÷ 7 = _____   45 ÷ 5 = _____   66 ÷ 6 = _____

Ending Blend -mp

Add the ending blend **mp** to each set of letters. Say the words.

1. bu _____   **2.** ca _____   **3.** stu _____   **4.** lu _____

5. swa _____   **6.** shri _____   **7.** pu _____   **8.** cla _____

Look at each picture. Circle the **mp** word that
names each picture and write the word on the line.

9.

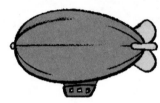

limp   blimp   skimp

_____

10.

jump   pump   lump

_____

11.

camp   lamp   ramp

_____

Sequencing

Read the poem below to find out what was wrong with Buzzy's car.
Read the sentences next to the poem. Decide what happened first,
second, and so on. Number the sentences in the correct order.

Buzzy's New Car

Buzzy saved up all his money
To buy himself a car.
The one he bought looked kind of funny
And didn't take Buzzy far.

The first time out, a tire went flat,
And the radiator cracked in two.
Then the engine broke down after that.
Poor Buzzy didn't know what to do.

He pushed the car off the side of the road
And hoped somebody would stop.
Buzzy was mad—enough to explode—
Then the other tire went, "POP!"

Now Buzzy's still sitting beside that old heap.
His hair all turned gray and grew long.
This one is a car nobody would keep.
Since everything on it went wrong!

_____ Buzzy's hair turned gray.

_____ The engine broke down.

_____ Buzzy bought a car.

_____ A second tire went "POP!"

_____ Buzzy saved his money.

_____ The radiator cracked.

_____ Buzzy pushed the car off the road.

Division Facts 8-9

Solve each problem. Write the answer on the line provided.

A. $16 \div 8 =$ _____ $24 \div 8 =$ _____ $54 \div 9 =$ _____

B. $36 \div 9 =$ _____ $72 \div 9 =$ _____ $56 \div 8 =$ _____

C. $88 \div 8 =$ _____ $32 \div 8 =$ _____ $72 \div 8 =$ _____

D. $45 \div 9 =$ _____ $81 \div 9 =$ _____ $80 \div 8 =$ _____

E. $27 \div 9 =$ _____ $90 \div 9 =$ _____ $96 \div 8 =$ _____

F. $40 \div 8 =$ _____ $64 \div 8 =$ _____ $63 \div 9 =$ _____

G. $8 \div 8 =$ _____ $18 \div 9 =$ _____ $108 \div 9 =$ _____

H. $48 \div 8 =$ _____ $9 \div 9 =$ _____ $99 \div 9 =$ _____

Division Facts 1-9

Divide to solve the problems and then color.

4 = red **7** = orange
5 = purple **8** = yellow
6 = green **9** = black

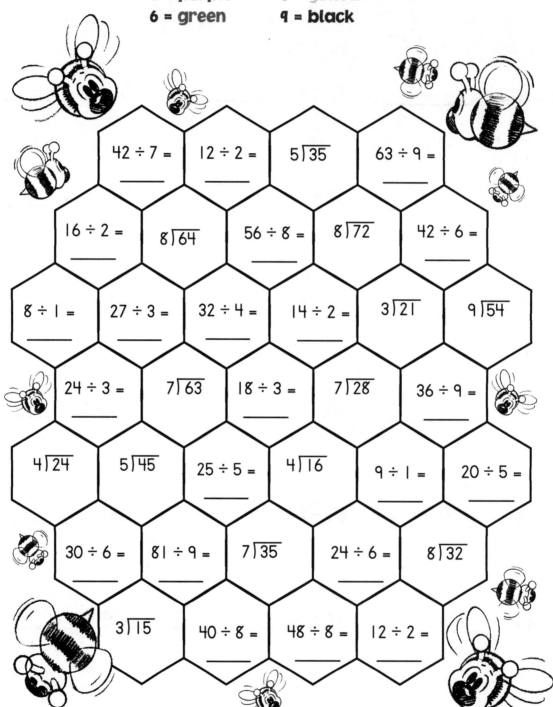

$42 \div 7 =$

$12 \div 2 =$

$5\overline{)35}$

$63 \div 9 =$

$16 \div 2 =$

$8\overline{)64}$

$56 \div 8 =$

$8\overline{)72}$

$42 \div 6 =$

$8 \div 1 =$

$27 \div 3 =$

$32 \div 4 =$

$14 \div 2 =$

$3\overline{)21}$

$9\overline{)54}$

$24 \div 3 =$

$7\overline{)63}$

$18 \div 3 =$

$7\overline{)28}$

$36 \div 9 =$

$4\overline{)24}$

$5\overline{)45}$

$25 \div 5 =$

$4\overline{)16}$

$9 \div 1 =$

$20 \div 5 =$

$30 \div 6 =$

$81 \div 9 =$

$7\overline{)35}$

$24 \div 6 =$

$8\overline{)32}$

$3\overline{)15}$

$40 \div 8 =$

$48 \div 8 =$

$12 \div 2 =$

Writing Paragraphs

Choose an idea for your paragraph. Write the title, main idea, and details. Retell the main idea at the end.

Title of Paragraph

Main Idea

Details

1.

2.

3.

4.

Retell Main Idea

Use the sentences above to write a paragraph. Write the main idea, add the details, and retell the main idea. Indent the first sentence. Use capital letters and periods. Remember to give the paragraph a title.

_____

_____

_____

_____

_____

_____

_____

_____

Using a Thesaurus

A **thesaurus** is a book containing words listed alphabetically. Beside the words are synonyms for the words. When you are writing a report or working on a project and you have used a word too often, you can turn to a thesaurus for another word that means the same thing.

Example: catch—grasp, grip, clutch, seize, take, snatch, capture, clasp

Find other words that you can substitute for each word below. Think of your own words before you turn to your thesaurus.

1. win _____

2. admire _____

3. vanish _____

4. bright _____

5. thin _____

6. calm _____

7. sleep _____

8. big _____

9. work _____

10. rare _____

Beat the Clock (Division Facts 1–9)

A.

$5\overline{)10}$ $4\overline{)28}$ $2\overline{)4}$ $9\overline{)63}$ $6\overline{)30}$ $4\overline{)16}$ $9\overline{)0}$ $3\overline{)15}$ $8\overline{)72}$ $6\overline{)18}$

B.

$8\overline{)48}$ $3\overline{)6}$ $7\overline{)21}$ $1\overline{)3}$ $7\overline{)56}$ $6\overline{)0}$ $2\overline{)16}$ $6\overline{)54}$ $1\overline{)7}$ $9\overline{)45}$

C.

$7\overline{)49}$ $5\overline{)35}$ $3\overline{)24}$ $7\overline{)7}$ $3\overline{)12}$ $8\overline{)24}$ $1\overline{)1}$ $9\overline{)72}$ $7\overline{)35}$ $5\overline{)25}$

D.

$9\overline{)27}$ $1\overline{)0}$ $8\overline{)40}$ $5\overline{)15}$ $2\overline{)2}$ $6\overline{)48}$ $5\overline{)0}$ $4\overline{)24}$ $2\overline{)8}$ $5\overline{)15}$

E.

$7\overline{)49}$ $6\overline{)12}$ $3\overline{)3}$ $2\overline{)12}$ $9\overline{)9}$ $1\overline{)5}$ $6\overline{)24}$ $4\overline{)4}$ $8\overline{)64}$ $5\overline{)45}$

F.

$2\overline{)6}$ $6\overline{)24}$ $4\overline{)12}$ $3\overline{)0}$ $8\overline{)8}$ $4\overline{)36}$ $2\overline{)0}$ $7\overline{)28}$ $9\overline{)63}$ $3\overline{)21}$

G.

$6\overline{)42}$ $7\overline{)35}$ $1\overline{)8}$ $9\overline{)54}$ $3\overline{)27}$ $4\overline{)0}$ $5\overline{)5}$ $5\overline{)40}$ $1\overline{)4}$ $7\overline{)0}$

H.

$4\overline{)32}$ $2\overline{)18}$ $9\overline{)81}$ $8\overline{)56}$ $3\overline{)9}$ $1\overline{)3}$ $2\overline{)14}$ $9\overline{)36}$ $4\overline{)8}$ $8\overline{)16}$

I.

$7\overline{)14}$ $8\overline{)48}$ $5\overline{)20}$ $6\overline{)6}$ $1\overline{)2}$ $8\overline{)0}$ $5\overline{)30}$ $7\overline{)56}$ $1\overline{)9}$ $8\overline{)32}$

J.

$1\overline{)6}$ $6\overline{)54}$ $6\overline{)36}$ $3\overline{)18}$ $7\overline{)63}$ $4\overline{)8}$ $2\overline{)10}$ $7\overline{)42}$ $9\overline{)18}$ $4\overline{)20}$

Time: _____   **Number correct:** _____

Ending Blend -nd

Look at the pictures and say the words.
Circle the **nd** word that names each picture.

1.

sand   fond   wand

2.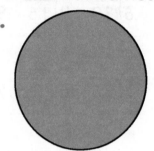

land   stand   round

3.

bond   band   bend

Read each sentence. Circle the **nd** word that completes the sentence.

4. We left at the _____ of the movie.   land   end   suspend
5. Be careful when you _____ on the stool.   remind   stand   hand
6. I saw a penny on the _____.   wind   send   ground
7. Guide dogs help the _____.   blind   spend   fund

Decimal Place Value

Rule:

The decimal point separates the ones digit from the tenths digit.

Example:

23.45 =	2	3	4	5
	tens	ones •	tenths	hundredths

Underline the digit in the tenths place.

A. 38.15   **B.** 11.18   **C.** 65.56   **D.** 50.63

E. 10.93   **F.** 9.95   **G.** 19.81   **H.** 19.58

Underline the digit in the hundredths place.

I. 19.62   **J.** 6.78   **K.** 73.17   **L.** 35.18

M. 25.84   **N.** 22.15   **O.** 99.99   **P.** 18.33

Proofreading

Add punctuation marks and capital letters where they are
needed in the story below. Add an ending to the story.

the mother bird was busy with her three new babies they were
growing so quickly soon they would begin flying they were always
hungry she could never seem to find enough food to keep them full
back and forth she flew all day long with worms and bugs

chirpy was the smallest of the three babies he was also the bravest
he liked to jump to the edge of the nest to see his new world the mother
bird warned him to be careful she said that he might fall from the nest
there were cats in the yard below how would he get home if he fell out
of the nest

the mother bird flew away to get the babies their dinner chirpy
hopped right up on the edge of the nest suddenly his foot slipped he
began to fall and . . .

_____

_____

_____

_____

_____

_____

_____

_____

Finish the Story

Hannah loved monster movies. She would stay up all night to watch them. One night when there was school the next day, Hannah sneaked downstairs to watch a monster movie at three o'clock in the morning. She was very tired when she went back to bed. When her alarm went off an hour later, Hannah got up and looked in the mirror.

"Oh, no!" she said, for now she was big and green and scaly and horrible. Hannah had turned into a monster herself.

Write what happened next.

_____

_____

_____

_____

_____

_____

_____

Vocabulary Assessment

Read the first part of each sentence. Choose the word that means
about the same thing as the highlighted word or phrase.
Fill in the circle next to the correct answer.

1. To **wash or clean by rubbing hard** is to . . .
   - ○ dimple
   - ○ crumble
   - ○ scrub

2. A **group of related sentences** is a . . .
   - ○ paragraph
   - ○ sniffle
   - ○ mission

3. When you **get something**, you . . .
   - ○ reappear
   - ○ navigate
   - ○ receive

4. The **smallest amount** is the . . .
   - ○ rate
   - ○ mutter
   - ○ least

5. Two things that are **completely different** are called . . .
   - ○ onward
   - ○ opposite
   - ○ mischief

6. To be **thankful** is to be . . .
   - ○ necessary
   - ○ sloppy
   - ○ grateful

7. Anything that **happened before now** is the . . .
   - ○ future
   - ○ past
   - ○ native

8. A **book that lists meanings** of words is a . . .
   - ○ marvel
   - ○ represent
   - ○ dictionary

9. When you **stay behind**, you . . .
   - ○ remain
   - ○ hitch
   - ○ express

10. To **make a person do something he doesn't want to do** is to . . .
   - ○ force
   - ○ outwit
   - ○ link

Compound Words

Finish the story below using the words in the word bank. Write the compound words in the blanks where they belong.

backyard	fireflies	lonesome	moonlight	waterproof
campfire	flashlight	midnight	rattlesnake	weekend

Camping

Last _____ I went camping. I had a _____ tent in case it rained. It was great fun at first. The _____ were glowing in the bushes. I built a warm _____. The _____ was so bright I didn't even need my _____! About _____, I became _____ and a little scared. I thought I heard a _____ near my tent. Thank goodness I was in my own _____!

Parts of Speech

Read each sentence. List each word on the line beside the correct part of speech.

1. These berries smash easily.

   noun _____   adjective _____

   verb _____   adverb _____

2. Ten soldiers march together.

   noun _____   adjective _____

   verb _____   adverb _____

3. The big pillow belongs here.

   noun _____   adjective _____

   verb _____   adverb _____

Reading and Writing Decimals

Decimals are numbers used to represent fractions. They contain a decimal point. Change the numbers below from word form to decimals.

Example: six and five-tenths is written **6.5**

A. two-tenths _____

B. five-tenths_____

C. seven-hundredths _____

D. one and nine-hundredths_____

E. four and six-tenths _____

F. fifteen and eight-hundredths_____

Ending Blends: -lk, -nk, -sk

Say the name of each picture. Circle the word that names the picture and underline the ending.

1.

trunk

silk

task

2.

yolk

sank

desk

3.

walk

bank

ask

Circle the ending blend in each word.

4. k i o s k   **5.** f o l k   **6.** h u s k   **7.** t h i n k

8. f r i s k   **9.** w i n k   **10.** s u l k   **11.** b l i n k

12. t a l k   **13.** y a n k   **14.** b r i s k   **15.** s k u l k

Cause and Effect

A **cause** is the reason something happens.
An **effect** is what happens.

Example:
The cat scratched me because I pulled its tail.
Cause—I pulled its tail.
Effect—The cat scratched me.

Underline the **cause** in each sentence.

1. The rain started, and the boys ran for shelter.

2. Mother served ice cream and cake after dinner because it is my favorite dessert.

3. Since I cannot swim, my dad will not let me go to the lake by myself.

4. Joshua sleeps most of the day because he is a baby.

5. Mary cannot go to school because she is sick.

Circle the **effect** in each sentence.

6. Noel went to the movies this afternoon because she was bored.

7. I was so tired that I went to bed early last night.

8. Since she had work to do, Anna did not watch television today.

9. I made an A on my test because I studied.

10. I skinned my knee when I fell off my bike.

Crossword Puzzles

1

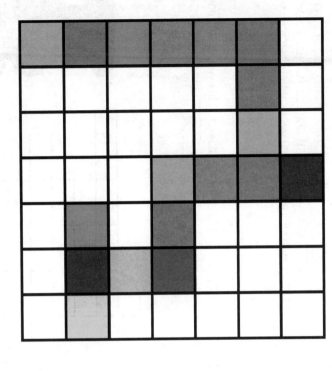

Use the word list to solve the crossword puzzle.

Word List

dragon	moat	queen
knight	armor	jester
king	castle	farmers

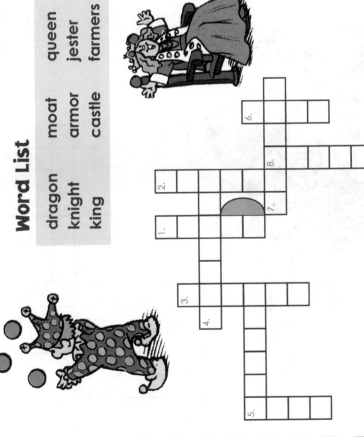

Across

4. _____ were people who grew food for the king.
5. A _____ carried a sword and served the king.
7. A _____ was a legendary fire-breathing creature.

Down

1. The wife of the king was called the _____.
2. A _____ amused the king by clowning and joking.
3. The king's large stone home was called a _____.
5. The ruler of the land was called the _____.
6. The water-filled area that surrounded the castle was called the _____.
8. A metal suit worn by a knight was called _____.

3

111

Use the word list to solve the crossword puzzle.

Word List

grizzly	cave
forest	claws
hibernate	grizzly
cubs	teddy
growl	

Across

4. Bears have sharp _____.
6. Bears sleep, or _____, all winter.
8. A large brownish bear found in North America is a _____.

Down

1. A wooded place where bears live is a _____.
2. A bear might make its home in a _____.
3. Baby bears are called _____.
5. A _____ is a noise a bear makes.
7. A toy bear with stuffing inside is called a _____ bear.

2

Use the word list to solve the crossword puzzle.

Word List

dessert	
waiter	
meals	
chef	
restaurant	
salad	
napkin	
beverage	
utensils	

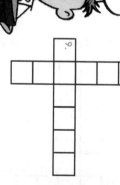

Across

5. A place to go out to eat is a _____.
8. Chocolate cake is my favorite _____.
9. Wipe your mouth with a _____.

Down

1. The _____ works in the kitchen preparing meals.
2. Breakfast, lunch, and dinner are all _____.
3. I like ranch dressing on my _____.
4. Knives, forks, and spoons are all _____.
6. A _____ takes orders in a restaurant.
7. Another word for drink is _____.

4

Use the word list to solve the crossword puzzle.

Word List

pool
water
goggles
raft
ocean
bubbles
kick
dive
stroke
splash

Across

2. Swimmers use their legs to _____.
4. A person wears _____ over his eyes to help him see underwater.
7. Air _____ float to the surface of the water.
9. A _____ can be used to ride on the waves.
10. The large body of water at the beach is called the _____.

Down

1. You _____ into the water when you jump head first.
3. A large container with water for swimming is called a _____.
5. A swimmer's arm motion is called a _____.
6. Don't dive into the pool if you don't know the depth of the _____.
8. Jumping into water causes a _____.

5

Use the word list to solve the crossword puzzle.

Word List

hail
clouds
sunshine
fog
rain
storm
wind
thunder
tornado
blizzard

Across

2. The _____ feels warm.
3. Wind along with rain, thunder, and lightning is usually called a _____.
6. It's snowing so hard I can't see. This is called a _____.
8. Water falling from the sky is _____.
9. March is a month with strong _____.
10. A cloud near the ground that is hard to see through is called _____.

Down

1. Boom! It must be _____.
4. A funnel of wind is called a _____.
5. Before a storm, you usually see many _____.
7. Rain in the form of small, frozen pellets is _____.

7

113

Use the word list to solve the crossword puzzle.

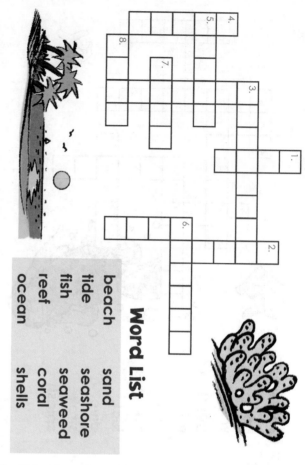

Word List

beach	sand
tide	seashore
fish	seaweed
reef	coral
ocean	shells

Across

3. Another name for the coast is the _____.
5. A marine animal that looks like a colorful rock is _____.
6. Many people like to walk along the beach and collect _____.
7. A _____ is a ridge of rock or coral near the surface of the water.
8. The rise and fall of the sea is called the _____.

Down

1. Many different types of _____ swim in the sea.
2. A _____ is covered with sand.
3. A _____ is a plant that grows in the ocean.
4. A large body of salt water is called an _____.
6. The beach is made of tiny grains of rock called _____.

Use the word list to solve the crossword puzzle.

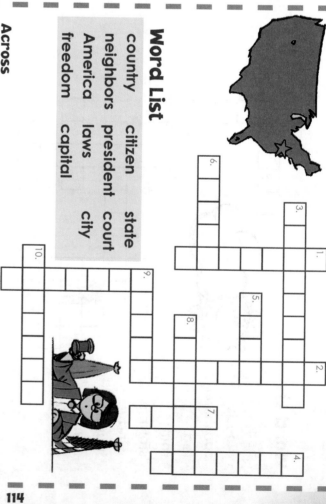

Word List

country	citizen	state
neighbors	president	court
America	laws	city
freedom	capital	

Across

3. People who live near you are your _____.
5. Rules that all citizens must follow are called _____.
6. Each star on the U.S. flag represents one _____.
8. U.S.A. stands for the United States of _____.
9. A judge hears trials in a _____.
10. Personal _____ means that citizens can make their own decisions.

Down

1. A person born in the U.S. is called a _____ of the country.
2. The chief executive of the U.S. is the _____.
4. The city that is the center of government is the _____.
7. A population center within a state is called a _____.
9. Another name for a nation is _____.

114

Adverbs

An **adverb** is a word that describes a verb. Adverbs tell **where**, **when**, **how**, or **to what extent** (how much, how long, or how often).

Examples: You can have a snack **later**. (When?)
Are there cookies **here**? (Where?)
Mom makes cookies **easily**. (How?)
I **never** eat potato chips. (How often?)

Use your imagination to complete the story with adverbs.
Remember, adverbs tell when, where, how, or to what extent.

News travels _____ in my school. On the

day I won 100 ice-cream cone coupons, _____

everybody was my friend. Marty came _____

up to me. She begged me for a chocolate cone. I told her ____

_____ that I would think about it. Fernando came

_____. He got _____ on

his knees and begged _____. Jill offered to

trade me her bubble gum for a strawberry ice cream coupon, but

I said, "No, thanks." Wow, people sure act _____

sometimes. I _____ do want to share my ice

cream, I just want to wait _____.

Ending Blends: -ft, -nt, -st

Say the name of each picture.
Write the ending blends, **ft**, **nt**, or **st,** to complete the word.

1.

li _____

2.

fore _____

3.

te _____

4.

pla _____

5.

a _____

6.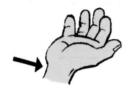

wri _____

7.

gi _____

8.

ne _____

Adding and Subtracting Decimals

Rule:

1. Line up the decimal points.
2. Start from the far right.
3. Regroup as needed.
4. Bring the decimal point down to the answer.

Example:

3.76 + 1.59 =

$$\begin{array}{r} 3.76 \\ + 1.59 \\ \hline \end{array}$$

$$\begin{array}{r} 3.76 \\ + 1.59 \\ \hline 535 \end{array}$$

$$\begin{array}{r} 3.76 \\ + 1.59 \\ \hline 5.35 \end{array}$$

A.
$$\begin{array}{r} 6.5 \\ + 7.3 \\ \hline \end{array}$$

B.
$$\begin{array}{r} 2.7 \\ + 4.1 \\ \hline \end{array}$$

C.
$$\begin{array}{r} 6.5 \\ - 1.2 \\ \hline \end{array}$$

D.
$$\begin{array}{r} 5.9 \\ - 2.5 \\ \hline \end{array}$$

E.
$$\begin{array}{r} 12.5 \\ + 9.4 \\ \hline \end{array}$$

F.
$$\begin{array}{r} 0.42 \\ + 0.36 \\ \hline \end{array}$$

G.
$$\begin{array}{r} 2.41 \\ + 7.49 \\ \hline \end{array}$$

H.
$$\begin{array}{r} 5.7 \\ + 8.5 \\ \hline \end{array}$$

I.
$$\begin{array}{r} 3.8 \\ + 4.9 \\ \hline \end{array}$$

J.
$$\begin{array}{r} 10.5 \\ - 7.7 \\ \hline \end{array}$$

K.
$$\begin{array}{r} 4.13 \\ - 2.95 \\ \hline \end{array}$$

L.
$$\begin{array}{r} 0.28 \\ + .87 \\ \hline \end{array}$$

Persuasive Paragraphs

You must convince your mom to let you play in the rain.
Give your reasons. Then, ask again.

Title	
Question	May I . . .
Reasons	1.
	2.
	3.
	4.
Ask again	

Use the sentences above to write a paragraph. Ask the question, state the reasons, and then ask the question again. Indent the first sentence. Use capital letters and periods. Remember to give your paragraph a title.

_____

_____

_____

_____

_____

_____

_____

_____

Syllables

Find out how many syllables are in each word by counting the number of vowels you hear when you say the word. Write the number on the blank.

1. machine _____
2. somersault _____
3. peanut _____

4. neighborhood _____
5. astronaut _____
6. koala _____

7. dragon _____
8. itch _____
9. hero _____

10. auditorium _____
11. longitude _____
12. congratulate _____

13. frog _____
14. multiplication _____
15. Canada _____

16. zipper _____
17. gulf _____
18. lasagna _____

Adding and Subtracting Fractions

Rule:

When adding or subtracting fractions with the same denominator:

1. Add or subtract their numerators.
2. Write that number over the same denominator.

Examples:

$$\frac{3}{8} + \frac{2}{8} = \frac{8}{8}$$

$$\frac{9}{10} - \frac{3}{10} = \frac{6}{10}$$

Solve each problem. Write the answer in the space provided.

A. $\dfrac{4}{7} - \dfrac{2}{7} =$

B. $\dfrac{1}{3} + \dfrac{1}{3} =$

C. $\dfrac{7}{8} - \dfrac{5}{8} =$

D. $\dfrac{3}{11} + \dfrac{5}{11} =$

E. $\dfrac{10}{25} - \dfrac{3}{25} =$

F. $\dfrac{1}{5} - \dfrac{1}{5} =$

Writing Stories

Write a story about the picture. Be sure to use capital letters and periods where needed. Give your story a title.

Things to Think About

Who is this story about?

Where does this story take place?

How does the story begin?

What happens next?

How will the story end?

_____

_____

_____

_____

_____

_____

_____

_____

_____

_____

_____

Division

Example:

$$6\overline{)30} \\ \,5 \\ \underline{-30} \\ \,0$$

Think:

6 divides evenly into 30, leaving no remainder.

Solve the problems.

A. $5\overline{)35}$ B. $7\overline{)14}$ C. $4\overline{)28}$ D. $3\overline{)24}$

E. $3\overline{)18}$ F. $8\overline{)56}$ G. $3\overline{)33}$ H. $8\overline{)64}$

Synonyms

Synonyms are words that have the same or almost the same meaning.
Examples: work – toil, small – little

Circle the two words in each row that are synonyms.

1.	beautiful	clever	pretty	eager
2.	wicked	evil	curious	calm
3.	hymn	honor	fall	respect
4.	sing	volley	clap	applaud
5.	get	return	area	receive
6.	unhappy	tender	shock	sad
7.	end	plead	beg	cause

Ending Digraphs: -ch, -sh, -th

Say the name of each picture.
Circle the word that names the picture and write the word.

1.
much
which
couch

_____

2.
brush
wish
dish

_____

3.
broth
with
mouth

_____

4.
wreath
bath
sloth

_____

5.
teach
peach
beach

_____

6.
rush
bush
ash

_____

Division with No Remainders

Example:

```
    1 2
4 ) 4 8
  - 4
    0 8
  -   8
      0
```

Think:

4 divides evenly into 48,
leaving no remainder.

Solve the problems.

A. 2) 64   **B.** 9) 90   **C.** 6) 72   **D.** 4) 100

E. 3) 69   **F.** 3) 36   **G.** 6) 84   **H.** 5) 125

Division with Remainders

Example:

$$4\overline{)35} \quad \begin{array}{r} 8\,\text{R}3 \\ -32 \\ \hline 3 \end{array}$$

Think:

35 divided by 4 is 8 because 8 x 4 is closest to 35 without exceeding 35.

Then, 35 − 32 is 3, and 3 is called the remainder.

Solve the problems.

A. $4\overline{)75}$ **B.** $6\overline{)63}$ **C.** $9\overline{)98}$ **D.** $7\overline{)87}$

E. $3\overline{)52}$ **F.** $8\overline{)89}$ **G.** $3\overline{)34}$ **H.** $2\overline{)39}$

Ending Digraph -ng

Read the **ng** words. Circle the ending digraph and draw a line from each word to its description.

1. b a n g   **A.** a piece of jewelry worn on the finger

2. f a n g   **B.** the part of a bird that helps it fly

3. r i n g   **C.** a sharp, pointy tooth

4. w i n g   **D.** a loud noise

Look at the pictures and say the **ng** words.
Circle the **ng** word that names each picture.

5.

hang   gong   sing

6.

wrong   king   long

7.

swing   lung   strong

Ending Digraph -dge

Read the words. Circle each word that ends with the digraph **dge**.

1. sludge
2. clay
3. partridge
4. insect

5. ridge
6. wade
7. fudge
8. age

9. lodge
10. hedge
11. sled
12. ride

Look at the pictures and say the words. Fill in the circle
next to the **dge** word that names each picture.

13.

○ badge

○ edge

14.

○ judge

○ fudge

15.

○ lodge

○ bridge

Problem Solving with Division

Solve the problems. Show your work.

A. Stan had 32 bags of popcorn to sell at the snack bar. He sold all of the popcorn to 8 customers. If each customer bought the same number of popcorn bags, how many bags did each buy?

B. Ms. Davis drove 325 miles in 5 days. If she drove the same number of miles each day, how many miles did she drive?

C. Phil sold 146 magazine subscriptions. He worked for 2 weeks and sold the same amount each week. How many subscriptions did he sell each week?

D. Reginald has 162 seeds to plant in his garden. If he digs 18 holes in the soil and wants to distribute the seeds equally, how many seeds can he put in each hole?

Problem Solving with Decimals

A. Complete the next 3 decimals in each sequence.

.15, .25, .35, .45, _____ _____ _____

3.8, 3.7, 3.6, 3.5, _____ _____ _____

B. Using the greater than (>) and less than (<) symbols, write two number sentences using the following numbers: **3.4, 3.5**

C. Place the following numbers in order from least to greatest.

2.5, 5.2, 4.2, 4.12, 5.25

_____, _____, _____, _____, _____

D. Chuck's weekly allowance is $5.00. After buying a package of beef jerky for $1.67, how much money does he have left?

Antonyms

Antonyms are words that have opposite meanings.
Examples: hot – cold, near – far

Circle the two words in each row that are antonyms.

1.	juggle	approve	explode	dislike
2.	grasp	fact	achieve	fail
3.	sure	blot	calm	stormy
4.	even	escape	plain	uneven
5.	wrong	call	wait	right
6.	shame	honor	helpful	below

Sequencing

Sequencing means to put things in the proper order.

The hot chocolate recipe in the box is all mixed up.
After reading all the steps, put the recipe in the correct order.
Some steps have already been written.

Hot Chocolate for Cold Days

Pour a cup of water into a pan and heat it until it is boiling.

Put 3 tablespoons of hot chocolate mix into the mug.

Pour the heated water into the mug and stir.

Place a marshmallow on top and drink.

Turn off the stove and remove the hot water.

Take out a mug, spoon, and hot chocolate mix and set aside.

1. Take out a mug, spoon, and hot chocolate mix and set aside.

2. _____

   _____

3. Put 3 tablespoons of hot chocolate mix into the mug.

4. Turn off the stove and remove the hot water.

5. _____

   _____

6. _____

   _____

Graphic Art Project

Follow the directions below to make a colorful drawing.

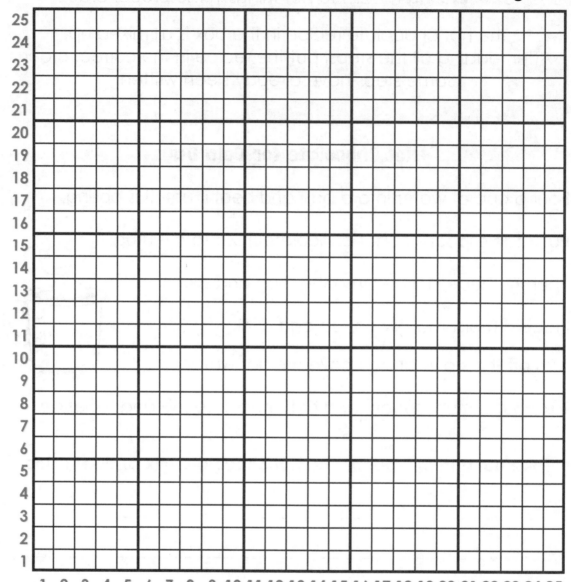

1. Color these boxes yellow: (10, 18) (10, 19) (10, 20) (9, 19) (11, 19) (8, 10)
2. Color these boxes red: (8, 1) (12, 1) Then, color the boxes between them red.
3. Color these boxes red: (12, 6) (12, 7) (13, 6) (13, 7) (9, 13)
4. Color these boxes brown: (9, 2) (10, 2) (11, 2) (9, 3) (10, 3) (11, 3)
5. Color these boxes blue: (10, 8) (10, 15)
6. Color these boxes orange: (6, 6) (7, 6) (6, 7) (7, 7) (11, 10) (12, 10) (11, 11) (12, 11)
7. Color these boxes green: (2, 4) (18, 4) Then, color the boxes between them green.
8. Color these boxes green: (3, 5) (3, 6) (4, 7) (4, 8) (5, 9) (5, 10) (6, 11) (6, 12) (7, 13)
                                 (7, 14) (8, 15) (8, 16) (9, 17) (10, 17) (11, 17) (12, 16) (12, 15)
                                 (13, 14) (13, 13) (14, 12) (14, 11) (15, 10) (15, 9) (16, 8) (16, 7)
                                 (17, 6) (17, 5)
9. Color the rest of the picture any way you want.

It's Me!

By _____

1

My name is _____

Here are some words that I
can make from the letters of my name:

_____
_____
_____
_____

Some interesting facts about my name:

_____
_____
_____
_____
_____
_____

3

This book is dedicated to

2

I Am Me!

I am unique, I'm one-of-a-kind.
My face, my body, and my mind
Are all special parts of me.
And there's no one else I'd rather be.
I like who I am, I certainly do.
I'm a special someone, I know it's true.
I am proud and happy to know
That I am ME from head to toe!

I am special because _____

Here are adjectives that describe me:

4

The _____ Family

This is how we look:

My Family

_____

_____

_____

_____

_____

5

My future is full of endless possibilities. I hope that when I grow up I can . . .

_____

_____

_____

When I grow up, I think I will look like this:

7

There's nothing like a good friend.
Some of my good friends are . . .

_____

_____

My friends and I like to _____

_____

Here's a picture of my best friend:

6

I can make today a happy day by . . . .

_____

_____

_____

8

Silent Letter in "tch"

Read the words. If the word ends with the digraph **tch**,
fill in the circle and circle the ending digraph.

1. ◯ pitch   2. ◯ search   3. ◯ hutch   4. ◯ fight

5. ◯ with   6. ◯ such   7. ◯ wrath   8. ◯ twitch

9. ◯ patch   10. ◯ hatch   11. ◯ fetch   12. ◯ clutch

Say the name of each picture. Circle the word that names the picture.

13.	14.	15.
		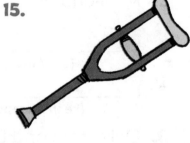
hatch watch catch	stretch itch blotch	batch crutch stitch

Perimeter

Perimeter is the measurement of the length around a figure.
You can find the perimeter by adding the lengths of all the sides.

Look at the following figures and find the perimeter of each.

A.

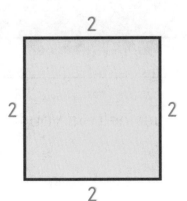

2 (top)
2 (left)   2 (right)
2 (bottom)

Perimeter = _____ units

B.

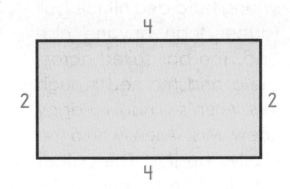

4 (top)
2 (left)   2 (right)
4 (bottom)

Perimeter = _____ units

Subject-Verb Agreement

Complete each sentence with the correct verb form.

1. In the summer, I _____ as a detective.
(work / works)

2. I _____ neighborhood mysteries.
(solve / solves)

3. When Mrs. Carter _____ her cat, I help her find it.
(lose / loses)

4. If there are footprints, I _____ out whose they are.
(find / finds)

5. My friend Jim _____ me secret messages.
(write / writes)

6. I _____ my decoder to figure them out.
(use / uses)

7. I _____ my detective kit in a secret place.
(keep / keeps)

8. Only Mom and Dad _____ where it is.
(know / knows)

Predicting

Read the paragraph. Then answer the questions.

The children were playing baseball in the empty lot. Peggy was at bat. She swung hard and hit the ball farther than anyone else had. The ball sailed across the lot and smashed through Mrs. Allen's window. Peggy knew Mrs. Allen would be really angry. The other kids scattered, running for home. Peggy looked at the broken window.

1. What do you think Peggy will do?

_____

_____

_____

2. Which clues helped you to decide?

_____

_____

_____

Metric Length

Rules:

1 centimeter (cm) = 10 millimeters (mm)
1 decimeter (dm) = 10 centimeters
1 meter (m) = 100 centimeters
1 kilometer (km) = 1,000 meters

Example:

Is 1 m longer than 120 cm?
1 m = 100 cm, so 1 meter is not longer than 120 cm.
Answer: No

Answer each question. Write **yes** or **no** on the line provided.

A. Is 15 cm longer than 1 dm? _____

B. Is 5 dm longer than 1 m? _____

C. Is 900 m longer than 1 km? _____

D. Is 1 m longer than 90 cm? _____

E. Is 1 m longer than 1 dm? _____

F. Is 20 cm longer than 1 m? _____

G. Is 5 mm longer than 1 cm? _____

H. Is 2 km longer than 1,500 m? _____

I. Is 2 cm longer than 10 mm? _____

J. Is 15 dm longer than 1 m? _____

Silent Letter in "kn"

Read each riddle. Write the **kn** word from the word list that answers the riddle.

knee	knife	knot	knapsack	knight	knoll	knocker

1. I can be found on a door. You use me to let someone know you are at the door. What am I? _____

2. You can put things inside of me and carry me. What am I? _____

3. I helped protect the king. I wore armor. Who am I? _____

4. I am part of your body. You can find me on your leg. What am I? _____

5. You must be careful with me. I help cut your food. What am I? _____

6. I am a small, round hill. What am I? _____

7. You can tie me in a piece of string. What am I? _____

Silent Letter in "wr"

Write the letters **wr** in front of each set of letters. Say the words.

1. _____inkle   2. _____eath   3. _____ong   4. _____angle

5. _____apper   6. _____eck   7. _____estle   8. _____ap

Say each **wr** word. Circle the picture of the word.

9. wrap	10. wrist	11. write	12. wring

Customary Length

Using an inch ruler, measure each line segment to the nearest inch.
Write the answer in the box to the right of the segment.

A. _____

B. _____

C. _____

D. _____

E. _____

F. _____

Customary Capacity

Rules:
- 2 cups = 1 pint
- 2 pints = 1 quart
- 4 quarts = 1 gallon

Example:
Is one cup greater than, less than, or equal to 1 pint?
If 2 cups = 1 pint
then 1 cup is **less than** 1 pint.

Complete each sentence using **more than**, **less than**, or **equal to**.
Write your answer on the line.

A. 2 pints are _____1 quart.

B. 1 pint is _____ 1 quart.

C. 3 quarts are _____ 1 gallon.

D. 3 cups are _____ 1 quart.

E. 1 gallon is _____ 1 pint.

F. 6 pints are _____ 3 quarts.

G. 2 pints are _____ 4 cups.

H. 8 quarts are _____ 2 gallons.

Silent Letter in "ck"

Read the words. Circle each word that ends with the letters **ck**.

1. jazz
2. speech
3. mask
4. crutch
5. rock
6. stick
7. click
8. lock
9. lake
10. quack
11. quick
12. sick

Read each word group. Write the **ck** word from the word list that belongs with the group.

Word List sock   stick   neck   quick   rock   truck

13. fast, speedy, _____

14. log, twig, _____

15. shoulder, arm, _____

16. stone, pebble, _____

17. shoe, feet, _____

18. car, motorcycle, _____

Silent Letter in "mb"

Say the name of each picture. Fill in the circle
next to the **mb** word that names the picture.

1.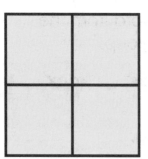
○ thumb
○ dumb

2.
○ climb
○ tomb

3.
○ lamb
○ limb

Read each **mb** word. Write a sentence using the word.
Circle the letters **mb** .

4. lamb _____

5. numb _____

6. crumb _____

7. climb _____

8. comb _____

Area

Area is the space inside a figure. It is measured in **square units**.
You can find the area by adding the number of squares in the figure.

Look at the following figures and find the area of each.

A.

B.

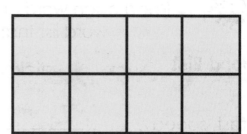

Area = _____ square units

Area = _____ square units

Reading a Map Grid

Sometimes a map is drawn with a **grid**. The number coordinates on the map grid below are located on both sides of the map. The letter coordinates are located at the top and bottom of the map.

Look at the locations of the different cities. Write the name of each city on the line beside the matching coordinates at the bottom of the page.

D–1 _____

C–2 _____

A–2 _____

B–3 _____

B–1 _____

E–4 _____

Area and Perimeter

Rules:

Area (A) is the number of square units inside a figure.
To find the area of rectangles and squares,
multiply the length times the width.

Perimeter (P) is the number of units around a figure.
To find the perimeter of rectangles and squares,
add the length of all four sides.

Examples:

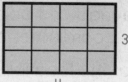

A = 4 x 3 = 12 square units
P = 4 + 3 + 4 + 3 = 14 units

A.

Area = _____

Perimeter = _____

E.

Area = _____

Perimeter = _____

B.

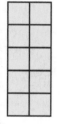

Area = _____

Perimeter = _____

F.

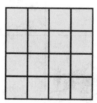

Area = _____

Perimeter = _____

C.

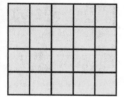

Area = _____

Perimeter = _____

G.

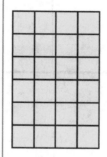

Area = _____

Perimeter = _____

D.

Area = _____

Perimeter = _____

H.

Area = _____

Perimeter = _____

Outcomes

An **outcome** is the result of an event.

Decide whether the following outcomes are **certain** (will definitely happen), **possible** (might happen), or **impossible** (will not happen). Write your answer on the line.

1. It will rain tomorrow. _____

2. You will grow to be 50 feet tall. _____

3. The Vikings will win the Super Bowl next season. _____

4. Tomorrow will be 24 hours long. _____

5. Humans will travel to Mars. _____

6. New Year's Eve will fall on December 31st. _____

Homophones

Homophones are words that sound alike but are spelled differently and have different meanings.

Example: tail – tale

Circle the two words in each row that are homophones.

1.	bear	seen	saw	bare
2.	violet	vase	vain	vein
3.	drop	dew	down	due
4.	tee	tell	told	tea
5.	well	weight	wait	went
6.	him	hair	hare	held

Reading a Map

Marcia lives in Flower City. She has a new friend named Tina. Marcia invited Tina to her house for a visit. Marcia drew a map to help Tina find her house.

Look at the map and use it to answer the questions below.

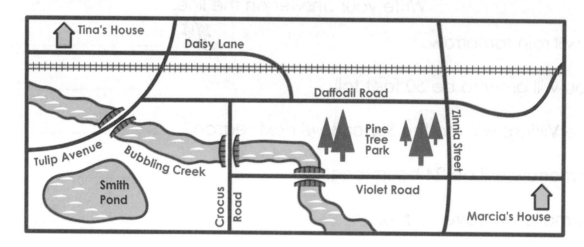

1. The road where Marcia lives is _____ .

2. The lane where Tina lives is _____ .

3. What four roads cross the railroad tracks? _____

_____ .

4. What road intersects both Daffodil Road and Violet Road?

_____ .

5. How can you get across Bubbling Creek? _____

_____ .

6. What roads intersect Zinnia Street? _____

_____ .

Punctuation

Place the correct punctuation mark at the end of each sentence in the story below. Write an ending to the story.

Making Pancakes

My sister and I woke early last Saturday morning   We decided to make breakfast for Mom   We took out the pancake mix   We put the mix in a big bowl   We added eggs and milk   I was stirring the batter   My sister was pouring orange juice   Then, the cat jumped onto the counter   He tipped over the glass of juice and knocked the bowl to the floor   Batter and juice went everywhere   Next . . .

_____

_____

_____

_____

_____

_____

_____

_____

Understanding What I Read

Read the story. Then, answer the questions.

Nightly Navigator

Many people do not realize what bats do for us. They are some of our best nighttime insect exterminators. Over 900 kinds of bats exist in the world today. These bats can be anywhere from one-half inch long to over 15 inches long. Although most bats eat just insects, some dine on fruit and the nectar of flowers. As the only flying mammals on earth, bats should be recognized for their contributions to humans. Aside from controlling the insect population, bats are the main pollinators and seed spreaders for many tropical trees like mangoes, guavas, cashews, cloves, and Brazil nuts. Bats use their sonar-guided mouths and ears to enjoy a nightly dinner of millions of mosquitoes, mayflies, and moths.

1. What is the main idea of this paragraph?

_____ .

2. How many different kinds of bats are there in the world?

_____ .

3. What do bats like to eat?

_____ .

4. How large can some species of bats get?

_____ .

5. What kinds of tropical trees depend on the bat for spreading their seeds and for pollination?

_____ .

How to Write a Friendly Letter

Review the five parts of a friendly letter.

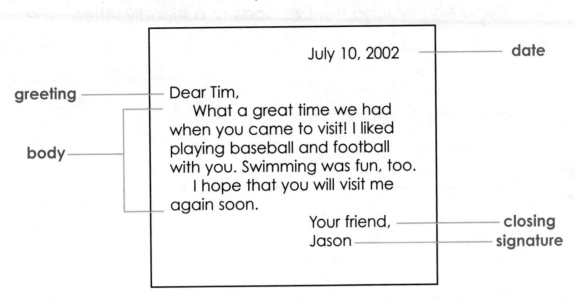

Write a letter to your friend. Talk about the things you like to do together.

_____
(date)

_____
(greeting)

_____

_____

_____

_____

(body)

_____
(closing)

_____
(signature)

Write a Friendly Letter

Write a letter to a new friend.
Be sure to include the five parts of a friendly letter.

Describe yourself.

_____

_____

_____

_____

_____

Tell what you like to do.

_____

_____

_____

Describe your room.

_____

_____

_____

_____

Describe your family.

_____

_____

_____

_____

_____

_____

Addressing Envelopes

Address the envelopes below using the information given.

The sender is:

Dr. James Madison
38 Carlton Place
Salem, NC 29532

The receiver is:

Ms. Mary Morton
149 Sparrow Street
Tucson, AZ 52974

The sender is:

Mrs. Alice Watson
9 Flag Avenue
Port Huron, MI 48060

The receiver is:

Miss Susan Coats
183 Spring Street
Denver, CO 50738

Answer Key

Short and Long Vowels Review
Phonics

Read each sentence. Listen to the first vowel in the highlighted word. Write ˉ or ˘ over the vowel and circle the correct word after the sentence.

1. Ray skied down the slōpe. **(long)** short
2. I put my picture inside a frāme. **(long)** short
3. The kīte was flying high in the air. **(long)** short
4. I asked Sean to tŏss the ball to me. long **(short)**
5. Ann picked a bŭnch of flowers from the field. long **(short)**
6. Tina is Marie's sĭster. long **(short)**
7. Put those papers in the trăsh. long **(short)**
8. I sat on the bĕnch in the park. long **(short)**
9. The tūbe of toothpaste was empty. **(long)** short
10. Put thōse books on the shelf. **(long)** short
11. I need to get out of the sun and sit in the shāde. **(long)** short
12. Lisa wore a white drĕss to the party. long **(short)**

Number Patterns
Math

Study each sequence of numbers. Circle the group of numbers that continues the pattern.

A. 1, 3, 5, 7, 9, . . .
   10, 11, 12, 13   **(11, 13, 15, 17)**   12, 14, 16, 18

B. 3, 6, 9, 12, 15, . . .
   (18, 21, 24, 27)   16, 17, 18, 19   30, 60, 90, 120

C. 1, 4, 7, 10, . . .
   12, 14, 16, 18   11, 12, 13, 14   **(13, 16, 19, 22)**

D. 1, 7, 13, 19, . . .
   21, 28, 34, 40   **(25, 31, 37, 43)**   21, 23, 25, 27

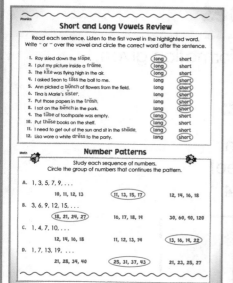
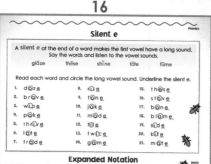

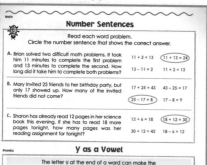
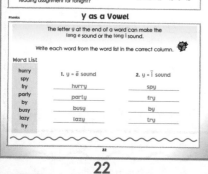

16

Ordering Numbers
Math

Rewrite the numbers in each row in order from least to greatest.

A. 6,283 683 561 656   561 656 683 6,283

B. 8,899 882 8,311 411   411 882 8,311 8,899

Rewrite the numbers in each row in order from greatest to least.

C. 737 3,778 7,138 397   7,139 3,778 737 397

D. 998 899 9,989 9,998   9,998 9,989 998 899

Long and Short Vowels Assessment
Phonics

For each word, write ˉ or ˘ over the vowel that correctly completes the word. Write the letter on the line.

1. wrĕck   ĕ u
2. sprŭng ŭ e
3. hōme   o ō
4. fĭlm   a ĭ
5. trăsh   ă e
6. chīme   ī e
7. scōpe   o ō
8. sīze   ī e
9. rūle   u ū
10. blāze a ā
11. cŏmmon ŏ u
12. tūbe   ū a

BONUS
Divide a sheet of paper into two columns. Write the long vowel words from above in one column and the short vowel words in the other column.

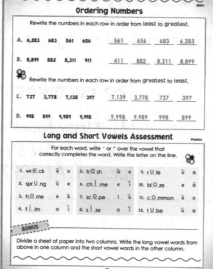

17

Addition Facts to 18
Math

Add to solve the problems in the problem list. Then, find the same problems in the puzzle. Circle the hidden problems and write + and = in the correct places. Problems are hidden across and down.

8 + 7 = 15	4 + 5 = 14	4 + 2 = 11	7 + 3 = 10	4 + 6 = 10
6 + 7 = 13	7 + 6 = 13	5 + 5 = 10	9 + 9 = 18	8 + 6 = 11
7 + 9 = 14	5 + 9 = 14	8 + 8 = 16	6 + 5 = 11	2 + 8 = 10
9 + 8 = 17				6 + 6 = 10
9 + 8 = 12				6 + 6 = 10

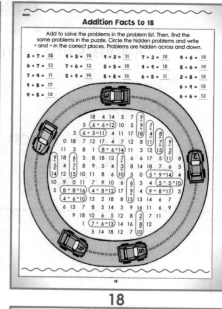

18

Silent e
Phonics

A silent e at the end of a word makes the first vowel have a long sound. Say the words and listen to the vowel sounds.

glāze   thēse   shīne   tōte   fūme

Read each word and circle the long vowel sound. Underline the silent e.

1. dōz_e_
2. brāv_e_
3. wīp_e_
4. pōk_e_
5. thrīv_e_
6. lāt_e_
7. trād_e_
8. rūl_e_
9. tōn_e_
10. jōk_e_
11. mōd_e_
12. twīc_e_
13. gām_e_
14. thōs_e_
15. stōv_e_
16. bōn_e_
17. blām_e_
18. sīd_e_
19. kūl_e_
20. māt_e_

Expanded Notation
Math

Look at the key and the model for a three-digit number. Then, fill in the missing information below.

Key
0 = hundreds
/ = tens
• = ones

Standard number: 482
Expanded notation: 400 + 80 + 2
Pictorial model: 0000 //////// ••

	Standard number	Expanded notation	Pictorial model
A.	327	300 + 20 + 7	000 // •••••••
B.	254	200 + 50 + 4	00 ///// ••••
C.	845	800 + 40 + 5	00000000 //// •••••

19

Fiction or Nonfiction?
Writing

Stories can be divided into two different types. Fiction is drawn from the imagination, and the events and characters are not real. Nonfiction has only facts about people, places, subjects, and events that are real.

Read the following paragraph and write fiction or nonfiction in the box.

Army ants are some of the most feared types of ants. These ants are very destructive and can eat all living things in their paths. Army ants travel at night in groups of hundreds of thousands through the tropical forests of Africa and South America.

nonfiction

Now write your own story. On the bottom blank line, write whether your story is fiction or nonfiction.

Answers will vary.

Try to think of a story character you would like to be. Draw a picture of yourself as this new character.

Pictures will vary.

20

Subtraction Facts to 18
Math

Subtract to solve the problems in the problem lists. Then, find the same problems in the puzzle. Circle each problem and write - and = in the correct places. Problems are hidden across and down.

Problem List
11 - 5 = 6
13 - 8 = 5
12 - 5 = 7
11 - 8 = 3
13 - 4 = 9
15 - 8 = 7
15 - 7 = 8
5 - 0 = 5

Problem List
10 - 2 = 8
12 - 8 = 4
11 - 4 = 7
10 - 7 = 3
4 - 2 = 2
9 - 2 = 7
6 - 4 = 2
18 - 9 = 9
12 - 9 = 3

21

Number Sentences
Math

Read each word problem. Circle the number sentence that shows the correct answer.

A. Brian solved two difficult math problems. It took him 11 minutes to complete the first problem and 13 minutes to complete the second. How long did it take him to complete both problems?
   11 + 2 = 24   **(11 + 13 = 24)**   13 - 11 = 2   11 + 2 = 13

B. Mary invited 25 friends to her birthday party, but only 17 showed up. How many of the invited friends did not come?
   17 + 25 = 43   43 - 25 = 17   **(25 - 17 = 8)**   17 - 8 = 9

C. Sharon has already read 12 pages in her science book this evening. If she has to read 18 more pages tonight, how many pages was her reading assignment for tonight?
   12 + 6 = 18   **(18 + 12 = 30)**   30 + 12 = 42   18 - 6 = 12

Y as a Vowel
Phonics

The letter y at the end of a word can make the long e sound or the long i sound.

Write each word from the word list in the correct column.

Word List
hurry
spy
fry
party
by
busy
lazy
try

1. y = ē sound	2. y = ī sound
hurry	spy
party	fry
busy	by
lazy	try

22

Schwa Sound (ə)
Phonics

Some vowels do not make a long or short sound. These vowels make the schwa sound. The symbol ə means a vowel makes a schwa sound.

Say the words. Listen to the schwa sound (ə) in each.

sofa (sofə)   lemon (leman)   father (fathər)

For each pair of words, underline the schwa symbol in the first word. Circle the vowel that makes the schwa sound in the second word.

1. system   syst_e_m
2. circus   circ_u_s
3. about   _a_bout
4. forward forw_a_rd
5. robin   rob_i_n
6. apron   apr_o_n
7. chorus   chor_u_s
8. camera   camer_a_
9. pencil   penc_i_l
10. letter lett_e_r
11. oven   ov_e_n
12. camper camp_e_r

Story Problems
Math

Read each word problem and circle the correct answer. Use extra paper to help solve the problems if you need it.

A. Marcia will run every day next week. If she runs 1 mile on Sunday, 3 miles on Monday, and 5 miles on Tuesday, how many miles will she run on Wednesday?
   9   11   **(7)**   13

B. John and Tonya went to the store to buy 2 boxes of oatmeal cookies. Each box has 12 cookies. How many cookies will John and Tonya have?
   (24)   36   48   16

C. Alex has 23 marbles. If Alex has 4 friends and he gives each friend a marble, how many marbles will Alex have left?
   27   **(19)**   4   20

23

Reading and Writing Numbers
Math

A number is usually written using digits in the appropriate place value spots. This is called standard form.

Examples: five thousand, two hundred fifty-one = 5,251
twenty-two thousand, thirty-three = 22,033

Write each number in standard form on the line.

A. six hundred thirty-four = 634
B. eight thousand, two hundred fifty-one = 8,251
C. nine thousand, three hundred twenty-two = 9,322
D. twenty-seven thousand, eight hundred = 27,800
E. seventy thousand, one hundred two = 70,102
F. eighty-three thousand, three hundred eleven = 83,311

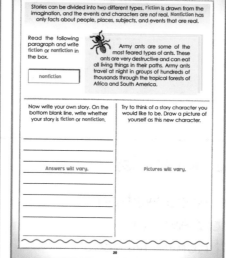
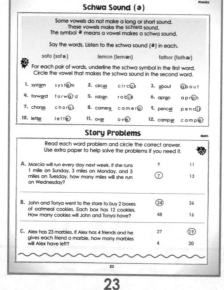

Beginning Blends: bl, cl, fl
Phonics

Write each word in the correct column.

flute blue clean clasp float fleet blimp blink cloak

bl	cl	fl
blue	clean	flute
blimp	clasp	float
blink	cloak	fleet

24

Answer Key

Expanded Notation
Math

Expanded notation is writing a number to show the value of each digit in the number.
Examples: 583 = 500 + 80 + 3
six hundred fifty-two = 600 + 50 + 2

Circle the letter beside the correct expanded notation for each number.

Eight hundred seventy-five =
A. 8,000 + 70 + 5
B. 800 + 70 + 5
C. 80,000 + 700 + 50
D. 800,000 + 70 + 5

Six thousand forty-eight =
A. 6,000 + 400 + 80
B. 10,000 + 6,000 + 400 + 80
C. 6,000 + 40 + 8
D. 60,000 + 40 + 8

Beginning Blends: gl, pl, sl
Phonics

Say the word that names each picture.
Circle the beginning blend of each word.

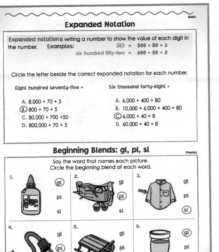

1. (gl) pl sl
2. gl (pl) sl
3. gl pl (sl)
4. gl (pl) sl
5. gl pl sl
6. (gl) pl sl

25

Nouns
Language Arts

Common nouns name any one of a group of things.
Proper nouns name a specific person, place, or thing.

Each sentence has one common noun and one proper noun. Write the common noun to the left of the sentence and the proper noun to the right.

Common Nouns		Proper Nouns
cousin	My cousin lives in Spain.	Spain
bear	Smokey is a famous bear.	Smokey
family	My family ate at Pizza Barn.	Pizza Barn
city	Ogden is a beautiful city.	Ogden
scientist	Isaac Newton was a scientist.	Isaac Newton
satellite	The first satellite was Sputnik I.	Sputnik I
camera	George Eastman made cameras.	George Eastman
months	The Pilgrims sailed for two months.	Pilgrims

Comparing Numbers
Math

Study the examples below. To compare each pair of numbers, use less than (<), greater than (>), or equal to (=). Write the correct symbol in each oval.

Examples: 375 (<) 6,200   7,000 (=) 7,000   3,482 (>) 2,843

A. 620 (<) 6,200
B. 493 (>) 439
C. 6,432 (<) 16,408
D. 9,286 (<) 13,489
E. 724 (=) 724
F. 3,080 (<) 3,800
G. 45,015 (<) 45,016
H. 397,124 (>) 387,425
I. 488,188 (>) 488,018

26

Two-Digit Addition with Regrouping
Math

Add to solve the problems.

A. 54 + 26 = 80
B. 44 + 39 = 83
C. 19 + 76 = 95
D. 24 + 47 = 71
E. 38 + 57 = 95
F. 29 + 64 = 93
G. 49 + 31 = 80
H. 78 + 12 = 90
I. 36 + 46 = 82

Beginning Blends: br, cr, dr, fr
Phonics

Say the name of each picture. Fill in the circle if the word begins with the blend in the box.

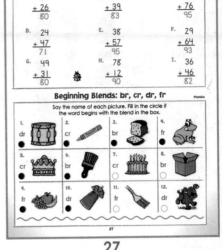

1. dr ●
2. cr ●
3. br ●
4. fr ●
5. cr ●
6. br ○
7. cr ●
8. br ●
9. fr ●
10. dr ●
11. fr ○
12. dr ●

27

Beginning Blends: gr, pr, tr
Phonics

Say the names of the pictures.
Circle the picture that begins with each blend shown.

1. gr
2. pr
3. tr

Read each word. Circle the beginning blend gr, pr, or tr in each word.

4. (pr)eview
5. (pr)oduce
6. (tr)uly
7. (tr)iumph
8. (tr)ead
9. (dr)op
10. (tr)ee
11. (pr)edict
12. (gr)ew
13. (gr)ound
14. (gr)uel
15. (gr)ant

Two-Digit Subtraction with Regrouping
Math

Subtract to solve the problems.

A. 70 − 19 = 51
B. 82 − 17 = 65
C. 70 − 22 = 48
D. 90 − 79 = 11
E. 78 − 59 = 19
F. 53 − 14 = 39
G. 66 − 8 = 58
H. 54 − 38 = 16

28

Pronouns
Language Arts

Circle the pronoun that completes each sentence.

1. _____ grew corn and tomatoes in his garden.
   Him   His   (He)

2. Please tell _____ what vegetables you would like to plant this year.
   we   mine   (us)

3. Tisha and _____ love to plant our watermelon seeds.
   we   (I)   us

4. Mother wants to plant flowers in her garden so that _____ will have something special.
   us   mine   (she)

5. We plant carrots, lettuce, and beans because _____ are good to eat.
   (they)   them   she

Addition with Regrouping
Math

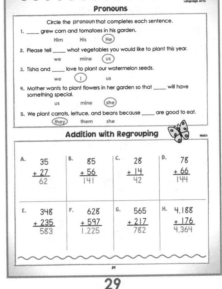

A. 35 + 27 = 62
B. 85 + 56 = 141
C. 28 + 14 = 42
D. 78 + 66 = 144
E. 348 + 235 = 583
F. 628 + 597 = 1,225
G. 565 + 217 = 782
H. 4,188 + 176 = 4,364

29

Adding Two or More Addends
Math

Keep the place values lined up to find the right sum. Solve the problems.

A. 62 + 27 = 89
D. 736 + 89 + 104 = 929
G. 6,428 + 1,375 + 3,684 = 11,487
J. 5,894 + 1,388 + 3,137 = 10,419

B. 75 + 85 = 160
E. 3,482 + 437 + 68 = 3,987
H. 30,147 + 25,236 + 42,613 = 97,996
K. 28,123 + 33,294 + 46,510 = 107,927

C. 54 + 92 = 146
F. 246 + 442 + 53 = 741
I. 2,804 + 1,366 + 5,391 = 9,561
L. 14,738 + 22,856 + 17,979 = 55,573

Beginning Blends: sk, sm, sn, sp
Phonics

Say the name of each picture. Circle the word that names the picture and write its beginning blend.

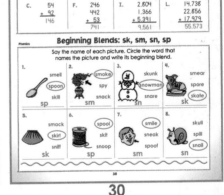

1. smell (spoon) skill — sp
2. (smoke) spy snack — sm
3. (snowman) spy snare — sn
4. smear spore (skate) — sk
5. smack (skirt) sniff — sk
6. (spool) skit snoop — sp
7. (smile) sneak snail — sm
8. skull spill (snail) — sn

30

Action Verbs
Grammar

An action verb tells what the subject of a sentence does.
Look at the action verbs in the following sentences.

Dino plays football in the fall.   We walk home every day.

Underline the action verb in each sentence.

1. Small airplanes fly over our house every afternoon at 5:00.
2. The rooster on our farm crows every morning at 6:00.
3. My dad plows the fields near our house in the spring.
4. The ducks in the pond splash water everywhere each afternoon.
5. Mother feeds the chickens twice a day.
6. My brother and I clean the barn every Saturday.

Two-Digit Subtraction
Math

Subtract to solve the problems.

A. 17 − 16 = 11
B. 46 − 25 = 21
C. 84 − 53 = 31
D. 78 − 16 = 62
E. 25 − 14 = 11
F. 27 − 13 = 14
G. 75 − 31 = 44
H. 68 − 14 = 14
I. 23 − 12 = 11
J. 42 − 31 = 11
K. 24 − 13 = 11
L. 82 − 71 = 11

31

Large Number Subtraction
Math

Solve the problems.

A. 52 − 39 = 13
B. 47 − 19 = 28
C. 61 − 25 = 36
D. 980 − 430 = 550
E. 543 − 298 = 245
F. 766 − 384 = 382
G. 7,303 − 3,855 = 3,448
H. 8,624 − 4,937 = 3,687
I. 5,322 − 1,404 = 3,918
J. 49,718 − 32,579 = 17,139
K. 38,972 − 24,687 = 14,285
L. 15,476 − 13,287 = 2,189

Correct Spellings
Language Arts

Look at the words in each row. Circle the correctly spelled word.

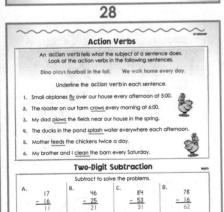

1. buzes   (buzzer)   buzzis
2. schol   schoul   (school)
3. sumtim   (sometime)   sometme
4. baloon   (balloon)   ballon
5. (work)   wrok   werk
6. monoy   (money)   monie
7. chaneg   chang   (change)
8. reding   raeding   (reading)
9. (homework)   homwork   homewrok

32

Syllables
Grammar

Answer the questions. Write the answers on the lines.

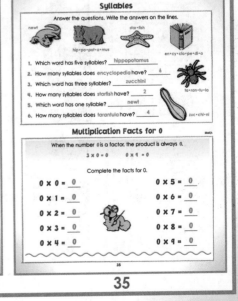

newt   hip·po·pot·a·mus   star·fish   en·cy·clo·pe·di·a

ta·ran·tu·la   zuc·chi·ni

1. Which word has five syllables? hippopotamus
2. How many syllables does encyclopedia have? 6
3. Which word has three syllables? zucchini
4. How many syllables does starfish have? 2
5. Which word has one syllable? newt
6. How many syllables does tarantula have? 4

Multiplication Facts for 0
Math

When the number 0 is a factor, the product is always 0.

3 × 0 = 0   0 × 9 = 0

Complete the facts for 0.

0 × 0 = 0   0 × 5 = 0
0 × 1 = 0   0 × 6 = 0
0 × 2 = 0   0 × 7 = 0
0 × 3 = 0   0 × 8 = 0
0 × 4 = 0   0 × 9 = 0

35

Answer Key

Page 36

Pictograph

The following pictograph shows the favorite pets of students in Mrs. Mill's third grade class. Each picture stands for one student's vote.

Favorite Pets

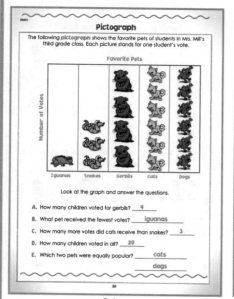

Number of Votes — Iguanas, Snakes, Gerbils, Cats, Dogs

Look at the graph and answer the questions.

A. How many children voted for gerbils? __4__

B. What pet received the fewest votes? __iguanas__

C. How many more votes did cats receive than snakes? __3__

D. How many children voted in all? __20__

E. Which two pets were equally popular? __cats__ __dogs__

36

Page 37

Multiplication Facts for 1

When the number 1 is a factor, the product equals the other factor.

$1 \times 9 = 9$ $2 \times 1 = 2$

Complete the facts for 1.

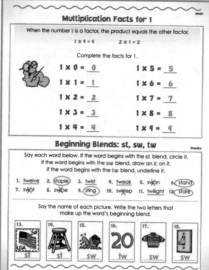

$1 \times 0 = 0$	$1 \times 5 = 5$
$1 \times 1 = 1$	$1 \times 6 = 6$
$1 \times 2 = 2$	$1 \times 7 = 7$
$1 \times 3 = 3$	$1 \times 8 = 8$
$1 \times 4 = 4$	$1 \times 9 = 9$

Beginning Blends: st, sw, tw

Say each word below. If the word begins with the st blend, circle it. If the word begins with the sw blend, draw an X on it. If the word begins with the tw blend, underline it.

1. twelve 2. (staple) 3. twist 4. tweak 5. swan 6. (stand)
7. swat 8. swipe 9. (sting) 10. sweep 11. twilight 12. (stare)

Say the name of each picture. Write the two letters that make up the word's beginning blend.

13. st 14. st 15. sw 16. tw 17. sw 18. sw

37

Page 38

Phonics

Beginning Blends: scr, spl, spr, str

Circle the beginning blend in each word below.

1. (scr)atch 2. (str)ide 3. (spr)inkle 4. (spr)uce 5. (spl)ay
6. (spr)ig 7. (spl)it 8. (scr)ibble 9. (str)aight 10. (str)eet
11. (spl)urge 12. (scr)oll 13. (str)eam 14. (spr)ay 15. (spr)ig

Use the beginning blend scr, spl, spr, or str to complete the name of each picture.

16. scrub 17. splinter 18. spring 19. scream 20. stroller 21. sprinkler

Multiplication Facts for 2

Multiply to solve the problems.

A. 3 ×2 = 6	B. 8 ×2 = 16	C. 0 ×2 = 0	D. 2 ×6 = 12
E. 2 ×5 = 10	F. 2 ×7 = 14	G. 4 ×2 = 8	H. 2 ×2 = 4
I. 2 ×9 = 18	J. 1 ×2 = 2	K. 2 ×8 = 16	L. 2 ×5 = 10

38

Page 39

Story Webs

Complete the story web. Use the words in the web to write a story. Be sure to use capital letters and periods. Think of a cool title for your story.

Things to Think About

Who is this story about?
Where does this story take place?
How does this story begin?
What happens next?
How will this story end?

cactus — hot — camel — desert

_____

Stories will vary.

39

Page 40

Multiplication Facts for 3

Use the sets below to help complete the multiplication facts.

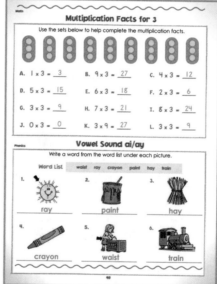

A. $1 \times 3 = 3$ B. $9 \times 3 = 27$ C. $4 \times 3 = 12$
D. $5 \times 3 = 15$ E. $6 \times 3 = 18$ F. $2 \times 3 = 6$
G. $3 \times 3 = 9$ H. $7 \times 3 = 21$ I. $8 \times 3 = 24$
J. $0 \times 3 = 0$ K. $3 \times 9 = 27$ L. $3 \times 3 = 9$

Vowel Sound ai/ay

Write a word from the word list under each picture.

Word List waist ray crayon paint hay train

1. ray 2. paint 3. hay
4. crayon 5. waist 6. train

40

Page 41

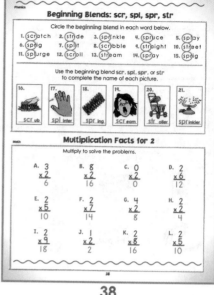

Word Searches

Parties!

Word List
party
celebrate
birthday
decorate
special
excited
surprise
invite
ribbon
balloon

41

Page 42

Success!

Circle the words from the word list in the puzzle below.

Word List
award
effort
special
students
achieve
success
admire
spotlight
deed

Sports

Circle the words from the word list in the puzzle below.

Word List
compete
field
referee
game
uniform
champion
overtime

42

Page 43

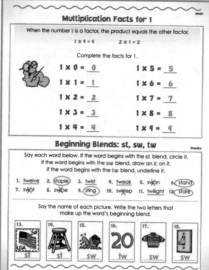

Bath Time

Circle the words from the word list in the puzzle below.

Word List
bathtub
bubbles
soap
clean
water
lather
splash
towel
scrub
washcloth

Air Travel

Circle the words from the word list in the puzzle below.

Word List
airplane
pilot
baggage
cabin
nickel
landing
depart
flight
hangar
tower

43

Page 44

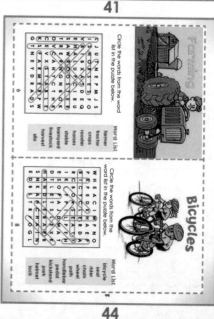

Farming

Circle the words from the word list in the puzzle below.

Word List
farmer
tractor
crops
rooster
stable
livestock
barnyard
harvest
silo

Bicycles

Circle the words from the word list in the puzzle below.

Word List
bicycle
seat
rider
wheel
chain
pedal
kickstand
spoke
helmet
lock

44

Answer Key

Punctuation Marks

Each sentence below is missing a punctuation mark.
Put the correct *punctuation mark* in each place that needs one.

1. Mario had a hamburger, some potatoes, and a milk shake for dinner. He can't eat another bite!

2. Mr. and Mrs. Blair went to the movies last night with their three children.

3. Did you know that Maple Ave. crosses Second St. at Main?

4. Dr. Barnes was able to see Mark yesterday afternoon.

5. José and Latasha visited Maine, Vermont, New York, and New Hampshire this past summer.

6. Is New York abbreviated NJ, NC, or NY?

7. Don hit two home runs in the game. His team won.

8. Wow! What a neat costume! I wish I were a pirate!

9. Benita thinks that she would like to be a doctor, but she also thinks that she may become a teacher.

10. Bernie's favorite ice-cream flavors are chocolate, vanilla, butter pecan, and maple nut.

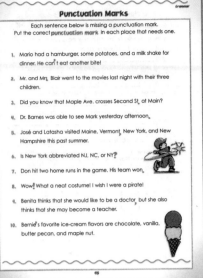

45

Vowel Sound ee/ea

Complete each word by writing the letters *ee* or *ea* on the line.

1. wh_ee_l
2. ind_ee_n
3. cl_ea_n
4. l_ea_ve
5. sp_ea_k
6. sn_ee_ze
7. tr_ea_t
8. sl_ee_p
9. s_ee_n
10. b_ee_p
11. sl_ee_t
12. tr_ee_
13. dr_ea_m
14. str_ee_t
15. gr_ea_se

BONUS

Write *ee* or *ea* to make each word match the clue.

st_ee_l (hard metal)   p_ee_k (to look)   w_ea_k (not strong)

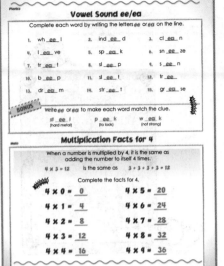

Multiplication Facts for 4

When a number is multiplied by 4, it is the same as adding the number to itself 4 times.

$4 \times 3 = 12$ is the same as $3 + 3 + 3 + 3 = 12$

Complete the facts for 4.

$4 \times 0 = 0$	$4 \times 5 = 20$
$4 \times 1 = 4$	$4 \times 6 = 24$
$4 \times 2 = 8$	$4 \times 7 = 28$
$4 \times 3 = 12$	$4 \times 8 = 32$
$4 \times 4 = 16$	$4 \times 9 = 36$

46

Multiplication Facts for 5

Use the sets of 5 below to help complete the multiplication facts.

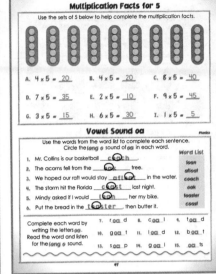

A. $4 \times 5 = 20$ B. $4 \times 5 = 20$ C. $8 \times 5 = 40$

D. $7 \times 5 = 35$ E. $2 \times 5 = 10$ F. $9 \times 5 = 45$

G. $3 \times 5 = 15$ H. $6 \times 5 = 30$ I. $1 \times 5 = 5$

Vowel Sound oa

Use the words from the word list to complete each sentence.
Circle the *long o* sound of *oa* in each word.

Word List: loan, afloat, coach, oak, toaster, coast

1. Mr. Collins is our basketball _coach_.
2. The acorns fell from the _oak_ tree.
3. We hoped our raft would stay _afloat_ in the water.
4. The storm hit the Florida _coast_ last night.
5. Mindy asked if I would _loan_ her my bike.
6. Put the bread in the _toaster_, then butter it.

Complete each word by writing the letters *oa*.
Read the word and listen for the *long o* sound.

7. r_oa_d   8. c_oa_l   9. t_oa_d
10. g_oa_t   11. l_oa_d   12. b_oa_t
13. s_oa_p   14. g_oa_l   15. o_oa_t

47

Vowel Sound ue/ui

Complete each word by writing *ue* or *ui* on the line.
Read the words and listen for the *long u* sound.

1. s_ui_t
2. cr_ue_l
3. s_ue_
4. fr_ui_t
5. br_ui_se
6. f_ue_l
7. tr_ue_
8. d_ue_
9. d_ue_l
10. n_ui_sance
11. cr_ui_se
12. j_ui_ce
13. cl_ue_
14. gl_ue_
15. T_ue_sday

Logical Thinking

Read the following word problems. Make notes to help you find the order of the people in each problem. Circle the correct answer.

A. Four marathon runners ran in a race. Use the clues to determine the winner.

> Mario ran faster than Shane.
> Shane ran faster than Randy.
> Tyler ran faster than Mario.

Who won the race?

a. Mario   c. Shane
b. Randy   d. (Tyler)

B. Davis lined up his four sisters by height. Use the clues below to determine the order of the sisters.

> Sally is taller than Kendra.
> Mary is the tallest sister.
> Trisha is not as tall as Kendra.

In what order did the sisters stand?

a. Mary, Trisha, Kendra, Sally
b. Mary, Sally, Trisha, Kendra
c. (Mary, Sally, Kendra, Trisha)
d. Sally, Mary, Trisha, Kendra

48

Main Idea

A paragraph is a group of detail sentences that support a *main idea*. The main idea is usually in the topic sentence at the beginning of the paragraph.

Look at each paragraph below and circle the main idea.
Underline the detail sentence that does *not* support the main idea.

1. Yesterday my class visited the zoo. We were amazed at all the animals that lived there. There were animals from all over the world in their natural habitats. I live in a house. My favorite animal was the elephant who lived on the African plains.

2. We played a game in our classroom yesterday called Silent Ball. To play this game everyone must stand in a circle and be absolutely silent. A sponge ball is then passed from person to person. The ball may be passed to a person next to you or to a person across the room. Mary does not like the game, so she chose not to play. If a player misses the ball or makes a sound, he must sit down. The last person standing is the winner of this soundless game.

3. José has an unusual pet. It is an iguana named Pete. Pete lives in a glass house made from an old fish aquarium. He eats a special diet of fruit and green plants. Sleeping at night and being active during the day is Pete's normal routine. My friend Martin has an iguana at his house, too. Pete has a greenish gray appearance and blends into his environment. José's unusual pet is fun to observe.

49

Beat the Clock (Multiplication Facts to 5)

A.								
$4 \atop 12$	$3 \atop 3$	$2 \atop 4$	$5 \atop 25$	$3 \atop 15$	$0 \atop 0$	$4 \atop 4$	$1 \atop 0$	$2 \atop 10$

B.								
$5 \atop 25$	$4 \atop 8$	$0 \atop 0$	$4 \atop 16$	$1 \atop 5$	$2 \atop 6$	$5 \atop 20$	$0 \atop 10$	$3 \atop 9$

C.								
$0 \atop 0$	$3 \atop 3$	$5 \atop 5$	$5 \atop 20$	$4 \atop 0$	$1 \atop 1$	$2 \atop 4$	$4 \atop 0$	$0 \atop 2$

D.								
$2 \atop 6$	$3 \atop 12$	$5 \atop 0$	$2 \atop 15$	$2 \atop 10$	$4 \atop 16$	$3 \atop 0$	$5 \atop 3$	$1 \atop 10$

E.								
$5 \atop 0$	$1 \atop 3$	$2 \atop 2$	$3 \atop 6$	$0 \atop 0$	$4 \atop 4$	$4 \atop 12$	$3 \atop 0$	$5 \atop 5$

F.								
$2 \atop 8$	$0 \atop 0$	$4 \atop 0$	$3 \atop 9$	$1 \atop 5$	$3 \atop 1$	$4 \atop 4$	$3 \atop 0$	$0 \atop 0$

G.								
$4 \atop 20$	$1 \atop 2$	$3 \atop 0$	$5 \atop 5$	$0 \atop 0$	$4 \atop 16$	$2 \atop 2$	$2 \atop 10$	$4 \atop 8$

H.								
$4 \atop 0$	$5 \atop 10$	$1 \atop 4$	$3 \atop 0$	$1 \atop 1$	$3 \atop 3$	$5 \atop 15$	$0 \atop 0$	$3 \atop 12$

I.								
$5 \atop 20$	$3 \atop 0$	$4 \atop 6$	$1 \atop 1$	$2 \atop 6$	$3 \atop 15$	$5 \atop 2$	$1 \atop 4$	$5 \atop 25$

J.								
$3 \atop 12$	$1 \atop 0$	$5 \atop 20$	$4 \atop 4$	$3 \atop 15$	$0 \atop 0$	$5 \atop 20$	$3 \atop 3$	$3 \atop 9$

Time: _____   Number correct: _____

50

Compare and Contrast

Fill in the blanks with words that tell how a cat and dog are alike and different. The first ones have been done for you.

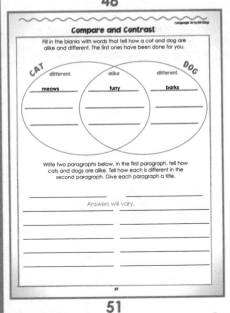

CAT — different: meows — alike: furry — different: barks — DOG

Write two paragraphs below. In the first paragraph, tell how cats and dogs are alike. Tell how each is different in the second paragraph. Give each paragraph a title.

_____   _____

Answers will vary.

51

Fractions

Fractions show parts of the whole.
Circle the correct fraction to answer each question.

A. What part of the drawing is shaded?
$\frac{2}{3}$ $\frac{1}{4}$ ($\frac{3}{4}$) $\frac{2}{4}$

B. What part of the drawing is shaded?
$\frac{1}{3}$ $\frac{1}{4}$ ($\frac{3}{4}$) $\frac{2}{4}$

C. Which fraction names the shaded part of the set?
$\frac{2}{4}$ $\frac{1}{4}$ ($\frac{3}{4}$) $\frac{2}{4}$

D. Which fraction names the shaded part of the set?
$\frac{1}{2}$ ($\frac{3}{4}$) $\frac{2}{3}$ $\frac{1}{3}$

Vowel Digraph oo

Compare the sound of the letters *oo* in the words *look* and *moon*.
Read each word and circle the matching sound.

oo = look   oo = moon

1. gloomy — oo (moon)
2. spooky — oo (moon)
3. crook — (look) oo
4. boot — oo (moon)
5. proof — oo (moon)
6. rooster — oo (moon)
7. book — (look) oo
8. foolish — oo (moon)
9. cook — (look) oo
10. wool — (look) oo
11. scoop — oo (moon)
12. took — (look) oo
13. stood — (look) oo
14. broom — oo (moon)
15. cookie — (look) oo

52

Identifying and Using Polygons

Circle the correct answer for each question.

A. Which figure has four sides?

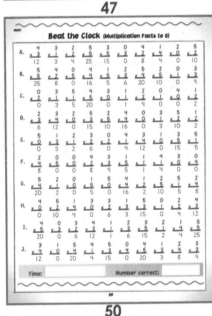

B. Which figure is a triangle?

C. What shape is the top surface of a can of soup?
triangle   square
(circle)   rectangle

D. Which figure can Roberto build using exactly seven squares?

R-Controlled Sounds: ar, or

Read each sentence. Write the correct word to complete the sentence. Circle the r-controlled vowel.

1. Sam is a good _sport_, so he shook hands with Mike after the game.
   (sport   sparf)

2. Our plane will _depart_ from the airport at 2:00.
   (depart   deport)

3. Our class will _perform_ a song in the spring concert.
   (perform   perfarm)

4. My brother and I are taking _guitar_ lessons.
   (guitor   guitar)

5. Ann walks her dog each _morning_ and afternoon.
   (morning   marning)

6. Rachel is my _partner_ in the science project.
   (partner   partner)

53

149

Answer Key

Symmetry

Symmetry occurs when two halves of a figure match exactly when folded together. The line of symmetry is the location of the fold.

Example: This square shows a *line of symmetry* from top to bottom (vertical).

In each group, circle the figure that has a line of symmetry.

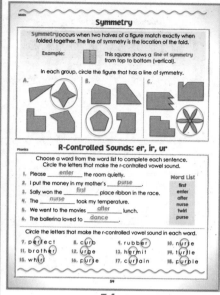

A. B. C.

R-Controlled Sounds: er, ir, ur

Choose a word from the word list to complete each sentence. Circle the letters that make the r-controlled vowel sound.

1. Please __enter__ the room quietly.
2. I put the money in my mother's __purse__.
3. Sally won the __first__ place ribbon in the race.
4. The __nurse__ took my temperature.
5. We went to the movies __after__ lunch.
6. The ballerina loved to __dance__.

Word List
first
enter
after
nurse
twirl
purse

Circle the letters that make the r-controlled vowel sound in each word.

7. p(er)fect   8. c(ur)b   9. rubb(er)   10. n(ur)se
11. broth(er)   12. (ur)ge   13. h(er)mit   14. t(ur)tle
15. wh(ir)l   16. p(ur)se   17. c(ur)tain   18. p(ur)ple

54

Multiplication Facts 0–5

Multiply to solve the problems in the problem list. Then, find the same problems in the puzzle. Circle the hidden problems and write × and = in the correct places. Problems are hidden across and down.

Problem List

1 x 4 = __4__
5 x 3 = __15__
3 x 4 = __12__
0 x 3 = __0__
4 x 4 = __16__
2 x 4 = __8__
1 x 2 = __2__
5 x 5 = __25__
3 x 3 = __9__
0 x 1 = __0__
4 x 5 = __20__
2 x 2 = __4__
1 x 1 = __1__
5 x 2 = __10__
3 x 2 = __6__
4 x 2 = __8__
4 x 1 = __4__
2 x 1 = __2__
4 x 3 = __12__

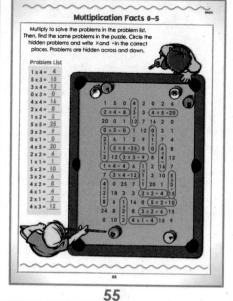

55

New Vocabulary Words

Use a dictionary to help you answer the questions below. You will have fun learning some new words and interesting facts. Look up the highlighted words and answer the questions on the lines.

1. Is a *goldfinch* a bag full of gold or a bird?
   __a bird__
2. If you were on a *jetty*, would you be on a jet or a wall along a waterfront?
   __a wall along a waterfront__
3. Is a *yak* a long-haired ox or a person that likes to talk?
   __a long-haired ox__
4. Would you draw a *parallelogram* or do gymnastics on it?
   __draw it__

Multiplication Facts for 6

When a number is multiplied by 6, it is the same as adding the number to itself 6 times.

$6 \times 3 = 18$ is the same as $3 + 3 + 3 + 3 + 3 + 3 = 18$

Complete the facts for 6.

$6 \times 0 = $ __0__ $6 \times 5 = $ __30__
$6 \times 1 = $ __6__ $6 \times 6 = $ __36__
$6 \times 2 = $ __12__ $6 \times 7 = $ __42__
$6 \times 3 = $ __18__ $6 \times 8 = $ __48__
$6 \times 4 = $ __24__ $6 \times 9 = $ __54__

56

Understanding What I Read

Read the story. Then, answer the questions.

The Wright Brothers

Orville and Wilbur Wright were famous American brothers. They owned a bicycle shop in Dayton, Ohio. Although they were interested in bicycles, they also loved the idea of flying. In 1896, they began to experiment, or try new ideas, with flight. They started by testing kites and then gliders, which are motorless planes. These tests taught them how an airplane should rise, turn, and come back to earth. The brothers made over 700 glider flights at Kitty Hawk, a field in North Carolina. This was fun but not good enough for them. Orville and Wilbur put a small engine on a plane they named *Flyer I*. On December 17, 1903, they took the first motor-powered flight that lasted about one minute. The brothers continued to experiment until they could stay in the air for over one hour.

1. What was the main idea of the story? Circle the correct answer.
   a. Testing new ideas is important.
   b. *Flyer I* was the first airplane.
   c. The Wright brothers were early pilots.
2. What does the word *experiment* mean? Circle the correct answer.
   a. to try new ideas
   b. to test kites
   c. to stay in the air for one hour
3. Where did the brothers test their gliders and plane? __Kitty Hawk, North Carolina__
4. How long did their first motor-powered flight last? __about one minute__
5. How did the brothers learn about what makes planes work?
   __by experimenting__

57

Diphthong au

Complete each sentence with a word from the word list. Write the word and circle the *au* diphthong.

Word List

| applause | vault | naughty |
| because | fault | caught |

1. The __applause__ was coming from the theater.
2. The bank teller got money from the __vault__.
3. We __caught__ ten fish on our fishing trip.
4. It was my __fault__ that we were late for the movie.
5. The __naughty__ puppy chewed up the shoe.
6. We did not have school yesterday __because__ it was a holiday.

Multiplication Facts for 7

Multiply to solve the problems.

A. 3 ×7 = __21__   B. 1 ×7 = __7__   C. 7 ×7 = __49__

D. 8 x 7 = __56__   E. 7 x 9 = __63__   F. 2 x 7 = __14__

G. 7 ×6 = __42__   H. 4 ×7 = __28__   I. 7 ×5 = __35__

J. 4 x 7 = __28__   K. 7 x 3 = __21__   L. 9 x 7 = __63__

58

Multiplication Facts for 8

Multiply to solve the problems.

A. 4 ×8 = __32__   B. 8 ×8 = __64__   C. 6 ×8 = __48__

D. 7 x 8 = __56__   E. 3 x 8 = __24__   F. 5 x 8 = __40__

G. 8 ×0 = __0__   H. 8 ×1 = __8__   I. 8 ×8 = __72__

Diphthong aw

Read each sentence. Write the correct word to complete the sentence.

1. We cut down the tree with a __saw__ (saw sau)
2. The farmer put __straw__ in the barn to keep the horses warm. (straw strau)
3. We stood under the __awning__ so we would not get wet. (awning auning)
4. The little __fawn__ could hardly walk. (faun fawn)
5. Put the meat on the counter to __thaw__ (thaw thau)
6. We gazed in __awe__ as the acrobat walked on the high wire. (awe aue)
7. My baby brother will __crawl__ before he learns to walk. (crawl craul)

59

Grid Coordinates

Look at the lines on the grid below. *Grid coordinates* are formed by the letters on the bottom and the numbers on the left side. If you look at the coordinates (C, 4), you should find the Enchanted Woods.

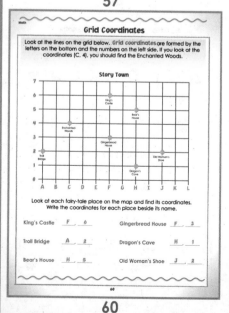

Story Town

Look at each fairy-tale place on the map and find its coordinates. Write the coordinates for each place beside its name.

King's Castle __F__ , __6__   Gingerbread House __F__ , __3__

Troll Bridge __A__ , __2__   Dragon's Cave __H__ , __1__

Bear's House __H__ , __5__   Old Woman's Shoe __J__ , __2__

60

Poetry—Haiku

Haiku is a form of Japanese poetry that follows a special pattern of 17 syllables. There are 5 syllables in the first line, 7 in the second line, and 5 in the third line. Most haiku poetry is about nature.

Read the following haiku poem.

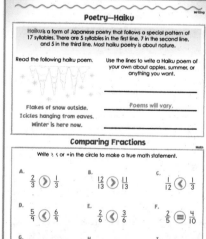

Flakes of snow outside.
Icicles hanging from eaves.
Winter is here now.

Use the lines to write a Haiku poem of your own about apples, summer, or anything you want.

__Poems will vary.__

Comparing Fractions

Write >, < or = in the circle to make a true math statement.

A. $\frac{2}{3}$ ⊙ $\frac{1}{3}$ (>)

B. $\frac{12}{13}$ ⊙ $\frac{11}{13}$ (>)

C. $\frac{1}{12}$ ⊙ $\frac{1}{3}$ (<)

D. $\frac{5}{9}$ ⊙ $\frac{6}{9}$ (<)

E. $\frac{4}{6}$ ⊙ $\frac{3}{6}$ (<)

F. $\frac{2}{5}$ ⊙ $\frac{4}{10}$ (=)

G. $\frac{1}{4}$ ⊙ $\frac{2}{8}$ (=)

H. $\frac{3}{4}$ ⊙ $\frac{1}{4}$ (>)

I. $\frac{3}{8}$ ⊙ $\frac{5}{8}$ (<)

61

Multiplication Facts for 9

Write the correct factor to complete each multiplication fact.

A. __4__ x 9 = 36   B. 3 x __9__ = 27   C. __2__ x 9 = 18

D. __6__ x 9 = 54   E. __5__ x 9 = 45   F. __7__ x 9 = 63

G. 1 x __9__ = 9   H. 2 x __9__ = 18   I. __0__ x 9 = 0

J. __9__ x 7 = 63   K. 9 x __1__ = 9   L. 9 x __5__ = 45

Alphabetical Order

Number the words in each group alphabetically from 1 to 5. You will need to look all the way to the fourth or fifth letter in each group before you start numbering.

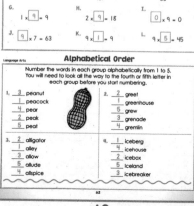

1. __3__ peanut
    __1__ peacock
    __4__ pear
    __2__ peak
    __5__ peat

2. __2__ greet
    __4__ greenhouse
    __5__ grew
    __3__ grenade
    __1__ gremlin

3. __2__ alligator
    __1__ alley
    __3__ allow
    __4__ allude
    __5__ allspice

4. __1__ iceberg
    __4__ icehouse
    __2__ icebox
    __5__ Iceland
    __3__ icebreaker

62

150

Answer Key

Singular and Plural Possessives
Grammar

Put an apostrophe in the correct position. Then, complete the sentence.

1. Several astronauts' spacesuits _____
2. That boy's football _____
3. The three poodles' fur _____
4. The four cats' claws _____
5. This week's laundry basket _____
6. My three friends' bikes _____ Sentences will vary.
7. The sun's rays _____
8. This robin's nest _____
9. The elf's voice _____
10. The two beavers' dams _____

Using Context Clues
Reading Comprehension

When you come to a word you don't know, use the **context clues**, or other words around it, to help you figure out the meaning.

Use context clues to figure out the meaning of each highlighted word below. Circle the correct meaning.

1. The green light coming from the haunted house was frightening. It was an **eerie** sight!
   a. green   b. (spooky)   c. funny

2. We must leave soon. We must **depart** as soon as everyone is ready.
   a. watch   b. (leave)   c. sign

3. The **clasp** of the seat belt was not fastened correctly.
   a. (buckle)   b. strap   c. seat

63

Using Prefixes
Grammar

A prefix is a syllable or syllables placed at the beginning of a base word to change its meaning. Here are some examples of prefixes:

un = not   re = again   dis = apart from, not

For each sentence, write a prefix that can be added to the highlighted word. Write the new word and its meaning.

1. I am **able** to do all of my work.
   prefix: _un_   new word: _unable_
   meaning: _not able to do work_

2. Mother will **agree** that my allowance should be more if I rake leaves.
   prefix: _dis_   new word: _disagree_
   meaning: _not agree_

Alphabetical Order
Language Arts

Number the names in each group alphabetically from 1 to 5. Remember to alphabetize names by the last name.
Do you recognize any of these authors?

A.
   _3_ Lewis Carroll
   _1_ Louisa May Alcott
   _5_ Mark Twain
   _2_ Hans Christian Andersen
   _4_ Charles Dickens

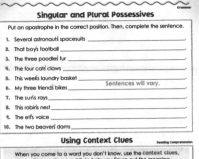

B.
   _5_ Jules Verne
   _2_ Edgar Allan Poe
   _4_ J. R. R. Tolkien
   _3_ Robert Louis Stevenson
   _1_ Sir James Barrie

64

Working with Money
Math

Read each problem and circle the correct answer. Use extra paper to help you solve the problems if needed.

A. Jarvis has 5 quarters, 10 dimes, 3 nickels, and 37 pennies. How much money does he have?
   $2.50 $2.67   ($2.77) $3.77

B. Michael has $6.25. If he rents a video game for $4.75, how much change will he have?
   $2.50 $2.75 $1.25   ($1.50)

C. Michelle wants to purchase an $11.00 baseball cap, a $15.00 shirt, and a $1.00 pack of gum. She has a $50.00 bill. How much change will she receive?
   $27.00   ($23.00) $77.00 $50.00

Diphthong ew
Phonics

Use a word from the word list to complete each sentence correctly.

Word List: knew   chew   threw   blew   flew   view   review   newspaper

1. Be sure to ___review___ the last five chapters before the test.
2. Juan ___threw___ the ball across the playground to Tony.
3. The ___view___ of the trees from the mountaintop was amazing.
4. I ___knew___ Susan would like the birthday gift you bought for her.
5. The ___newspaper___ is on the kitchen table.
6. Use your teeth to ___chew___ your food.
7. I watched the bird as it ___flew___ away.
8. The wind ___blew___ the papers across the street.

65

Entry Words and Guide Words
Language Arts

Entry words are listed in the dictionary.
Guide words are words at the top of each page in the dictionary.

Look at each entry word and the guide words beside it. Decide if the entry word would come between the two guide words alphabetically in a dictionary. Write **yes** or **no** on the line.

	Entry Word	Guide Word	
1.	pyramid	puzzle, python	yes
2.	acrobat	acme, action	yes
3.	tutor	twinge, type	no
4.	wrist	worsen, wrestle	no
5.	blob	bleach, block	no
6.	hummingbird	hunch, husky	no
7.	crimson	crime, crocodile	yes
8.	fill	file, film	yes
9.	injure	inherit, ink	yes
10.	silver	silly, single	yes

Look at the guide words at the top of each word list below. Circle only the words that would be entry words on a dictionary page with those guide words.

A. lead—lease   B. crocus—crossing   C. gift—globe   D. rude—rummy
(lean)   cricket   giant   royal
(leap)   (crop)   (give)   (ruler)
left   (croquet)   glove   ruin
(leaf)   (cross)   (glass)   ruby

66

Review Multiplication Facts 6–9
Math

Complete the multiplication facts. Do you see any patterns?

A. 6×0 = 0   7×0 = 0   8×0 = 0   9×0 = 0
B. 6×1 = 6   7×1 = 7   8×1 = 8   9×1 = 9
C. 6×2 = 12 7×2 = 14 8×2 = 16 9×2 = 18
D. 6×3 = 18 7×3 = 21 8×3 = 24 9×3 = 27
E. 6×4 = 24 7×4 = 28 8×4 = 32 9×4 = 36
F. 6×5 = 30 7×5 = 35 8×5 = 40 9×5 = 45

Diphthong oi
Phonics

Use an oi word from the word list to complete each sentence.

1. My mother put a lace ___doily___ on the table.
2. The elbow is a ___joint___ in the arm.
3. The students had to ___appoint___ a class president.
4. Plant the seed in the ___soil___.
5. I want to ___join___ the baseball team.
6. The singer had a lovely ___voice___.
7. The change purse had only one ___coin___ in it.
8. The water in the pot got so hot that it began to ___boil___.
9. It is hard to write well with a pencil that has a dull ___point___.

Word List: voice, point, join, doily, soil, appoint, joint, boil, coin

67

Diphthong ou
Phonics

Write each ou word from the word list under its rhyming word. Circle the ou diphthong in each word.

Word List: sound, sprout, pout, trout, stout, about, surround, shout, pound, hound

scout — sprout, pout, trout
mound — sound, bound, round, pound
mound — surround, hound

scout	mound
sprout	sound
pout	bound
trout	round
stout	surround
about	pound
shout	hound

Review Multiplication Facts 6–9
Math

Circle the correct product for each multiplication fact.

A. 6×7 = (42) / 12
B. 9×6 = 11 / (54)
C. 4×6 = (24) / 16
D. 4×7 = (28) / 40
E. 8×8 = 40 / (64)
F. 5×9 = 18 / (45)

68

Definitions
Reading Comprehension

Mary Martin, alias Peter Pan

Mary Martin is fondly remembered as the petite star who won an Emmy award for her performance in the TV production of *Peter Pan*. This cheerful, exuberant star was born Mary Virginia Martin on December 1, 1913. When she was 16, she married Benjamin Hagman. They had a son, Larry, who is renowned for his roles in the TV series *I Dream of Jeannie* and *Dallas*. Mary exhibited a talent for aerial ballet. After teaching and performing dance for several years, she journeyed to Hollywood to further her career. She had many roles in films and on Broadway.

Read the paragraph above carefully. Write the letter of the definition on the line next to each numbered word.

1. fondly ___d___   a. traveled
2. petite ___h___   b. job, occupation
3. performance ___i___ c. well known, famous
4. exuberant ___e___   d. lovingly
5. renowned ___c___   e. enthusiastic
6. roles ___g___   f. in the air
7. exhibited ___j___   g. parts or characters played by an actor
8. aerial ___f___   h. small, little
9. journeyed ___a___   i. the act of performing
10. career ___b___   j. showed or displayed

69

Reading a Table
Math

A table is a compact, orderly arrangement of facts or figures, usually presented in rows or columns.

Ross's Video Rental Review

Use this table to answer the questions below.

	Sun.	Mon.	Tues.	Wed.	Thurs.	Fri.	Sat.
Chuckle Chipmunk	1	4	0	2	3	5	2
Swamp Critters	2	3	1	2	0	2	3
Hero for a Day	0	6	2	1	4	5	5
Scary Vegetables	2	1	2	4	0	3	4
Halloween Howl	1	3	2	0	0	2	2

The numbers tell how many times each movie was rented each day.

1. Which video was rented the most on Monday? — Hero for a Day
2. Which video was rented the least on Monday? — Scary Vegetables
3. Which video was not rented on Tuesday? — Chuckle Chipmunk
4. Which video was not rented on Wednesday or Thursday? — Halloween Howl
5. Were more videos rented on Saturday or Sunday? — Saturday
6. Was Chuckle Chipmunk rented more than Halloween Howl? — yes
7. On what day were the fewest videos rented? — Sunday
8. Were more videos rented on Tuesday or Wednesday? — Wednesday
9. Which two days had seven video rentals each? — Tuesday and Thursday
10. How many times was *Swamp Critters* rented this week? — 13

71

Beat the Clock (Multiplication Facts Review)
Math

A. 9×1 = 9   5×8 = 40   2×5 = 10   7×5 = 35   4×7 = 28
B. 0×5 = 0   8×0 = 0   8×6 = 48   0×9 = 0   6×3 = 18
C. 9×6 = 54   7×4 = 28   4×4 = 16   6×0 = 0   3×0 = 0
D. 6×4 = 24   1×7 = 7   3×7 = 21   3×1 = 3   5×3 = 15
E. 9×9 = 81   9×3 = 27   0×4 = 0   7×9 = 63   6×0 = 0
F. 1×3 = 3   4×8 = 32   5×7 = 35   5×2 = 10   2×1 = 2
G. 9×4 = 36   1×0 = 0   7×1 = 7   0×0 = 0   3×6 = 18
H. 4×3 = 12   7×8 = 56   4×5 = 20   5×8 = 40   1×2 = 2
I. 3×8 = 24   9×8 = 72   5×1 = 5   3×0 = 0   7×3 = 21
J. 8×1 = 8   5×6 = 30   2×0 = 0   6×2 = 12   0×8 = 0
K. 9×7 = 63   0×1 = 0   6×6 = 36   1×6 = 6   2×9 = 18
L. 5×0 = 0   6×9 = 54   3×2 = 6   8×0 = 0   4×0 = 0
M. 7×2 = 14   2×6 = 12   0×7 = 0   3×5 = 15   4×6 = 24
N. 2×3 = 6   5×9 = 45   4×2 = 8   1×1 = 1   7×7 = 49
O. 6×5 = 30   0×6 = 0   5×5 = 25   9×2 = 18   8×2 = 16
P. 3×9 = 27   6×1 = 6   1×5 = 5   2×8 = 16   2×2 = 4
Q. 4×4 = 16   1×9 = 9   9×4 = 36   0×2 = 0   6×7 = 42
R. 8×4 = 32   4×5 = 20   7×6 = 42   9×5 = 45   5×4 = 20
S. 8×8 = 64   6×8 = 48   9×0 = 0   3×3 = 9   8×7 = 56
T. 3×4 = 12   4×1 = 4   2×7 = 14   8×3 = 24   1×8 = 8

Time: _____   Number correct: _____

72

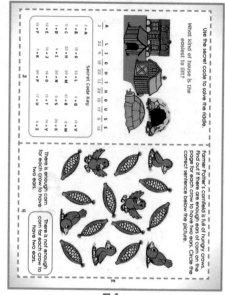

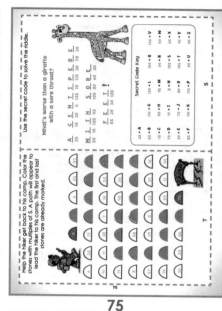

73

74

75

76

Multiplication Facts 0-9 Review

Problem List

Multiply to solve the problems in the problem list. Then, find the same problems in the puzzle. Circle the hidden problems and write × and = in the correct places. Problems are hidden across and down.

$9 \times 1 = 9$
$8 \times 5 = 40$ $5 \times 8 = 40$
$7 \times 5 = 35$ $9 \times 9 = 81$
$7 \times 3 = 21$ $3 \times 8 = 24$
$7 \times 7 = 49$ $4 \times 9 = 36$
$6 \times 6 = 36$ $3 \times 6 = 18$
$7 \times 4 = 28$ $0 \times 8 = 0$
$8 \times 4 = 32$ $9 \times 5 = 45$
$9 \times 2 = 18$ $7 \times 5 = 35$
$8 \times 8 = 64$ $9 \times 7 = 63$

77

Multiplying One- and Two-Digit Numbers

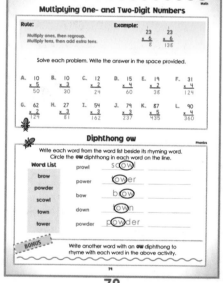

Rule: Multiply ones, then regroup. Multiply tens, then add extra tens.

Example:
$$\begin{array}{r} 23 \\ \times\ 6 \\ \hline 138 \end{array}$$

Solve each problem. Write the answer in the space provided.

A. $10 \times 5 = 50$ B. $10 \times 3 = 30$ C. $12 \times 2 = 24$ D. $15 \times 4 = 60$ E. $19 \times 2 = 38$ F. $31 \times 4 = 124$

G. $62 \times 2 = 124$ H. $27 \times 3 = 81$ I. $54 \times 3 = 162$ J. $79 \times 3 = 237$ K. $87 \times 5 = 435$ L. $90 \times 4 = 360$

Diphthong ow

Write each word from the word list beside its rhyming word. Circle the ow diphthong in each word on the line.

Word List: prowl, brow, powder, scowl, town, tower

prowl — scowl
power — tower
bow — brow
down — town
powder — powder

BONUS Write another word with an ow diphthong to rhyme with each word in the above activity.

79

Drawing Conclusions

Read the story. Then, answer the questions.

Photograph

Jack was not comfortable. His new shirt was too stiff and his tie felt tight. Mother had fussed over his hair trying to get it to look just right. She made him scrub his hands three times to get the dirt from under his fingernails! Finally, his mom said he was ready. She smiled and said that Jack looked very handsome. Jack frowned, but knew he could not tell his mom how he felt. This was important to her. Jack sat on a special stool that turned and looked at the camera. He didn't feel like smiling, but he did his best. "Perfect!" said the man behind the camera as he snapped the shot. Jack posed two more times and then the man said they were finished. The first thing Jack did was take off his tie!

1. What was Jack doing?
   He was having his picture taken.

2. What clues tell you where Jack is?
   sitting on the stool, looking at the camera

3. How does Jack feel about this?
   He does not want to do it.

4. What clues tell you how Jack feels?
   His shirt was too stiff. His tie was too tight.

5. Who was the man that said "perfect"?
   the photographer

6. Why did Jack take off his tie?
   It was not comfortable.

80

Counting Syllables

Syllables represent the number of vowel sounds heard in words.

Examples: what — 1 vowel sound and 1 syllable
pencil — 2 vowel sounds and 2 syllables
animal — 3 vowel sounds and 3 syllables

Read each word below and use the line to write the number of syllables in the word. Listen to make sure that the number of vowel sounds equals the number of syllables for each word.

1. apple — 2
2. prune — 1
3. cherry — 2
4. banana — 3
5. lemon — 2
6. pear — 1
7. watermelon — 4
8. plum — 1
9. strawberry — 3

Alphabetical Order

To alphabetize titles you need to put small words like A, The, or An at the end of a title.

Example: The Cat in the Hat would be Cat in the Hat, The

Number the titles from 1 to 9 as they should appear alphabetically.

3 Charlotte's Friend
1 Amos Goes Camping
4 The Chocolate Prize
5 Harvey's Mystery
8 The Whale Watchers
6 A Lion and a Bear
9 Where the River Ends
2 Cats for Sale
7 The Needlefish Return

81

Multiplying One- and Three-Digit Numbers

Rule:
1. Multiply ones, then regroup.
2. Multiply tens, then add extra tens.
3. Multiply hundreds.
4. Regroup as needed.

Example:
$$\begin{array}{r} 453 \\ \times\ 4 \\ \hline 2 \end{array} \quad \begin{array}{r} 453 \\ \times\ 4 \\ \hline 12 \end{array} \quad \begin{array}{r} 453 \\ \times\ 4 \\ \hline 1,812 \end{array}$$

Solve the problems. Write the answers in the space provided.

A. $100 \times 3 = 300$ B. $120 \times 2 = 240$ C. $278 \times 4 = 1,112$ D. $329 \times 3 = 987$

E. $422 \times 5 = 2,110$ F. $705 \times 4 = 2,820$ G. $827 \times 9 = 7,443$ H. $926 \times 7 = 6,482$

Understanding What I Read

What Eats the Firefly?

There are very few animals that are not eaten by something. No creature, however, eats the firefly, or lightning bug. The adult firefly has almost no predators. Birds, insect-eating mammals, reptiles, and fish do not eat them. Sharks are also bothered by them. They will swish around wildly and then seem to be paralyzed with fear when fireflies are put in their tank.

Read the paragraph. Then, answer the questions.

1. What is the main idea of the paragraph? No creature eats the firefly.
2. What is another name for a firefly? lightning bug
3. Describe what the fearless shark will do if a firefly is in its tank. swish around wildly and then seem to be paralyzed with fear
4. What do you think a predator is? Answers will vary.

82

Answer Key

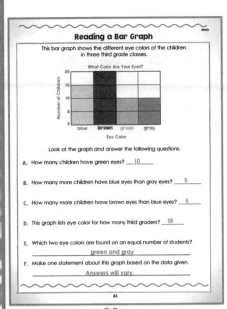

Reading a Bar Graph

This bar graph shows the different eye colors of the children in three third grade classes.

What Color Are Your Eyes?

Look at the graph and answer the following questions.

A. How many children have green eyes? __10__

B. How many more children have blue eyes than gray eyes? __5__

C. How many more children have brown eyes than blue eyes? __5__

D. This graph lists eye color for how many third graders? __55__

E. Which two eye colors are found on an equal number of students?
   __green and gray__

F. Make one statement about this graph based on the data given.
   __Answers will vary.__

83

Diphthong oy

Look at the highlighted letters in each pair of words. Circle the word that is spelled correctly, and then use the word in a sentence.

1. (enjoy)   enjoi   __Sentences will vary.__
2. destroi   (destroy)   _____
3. loial   (loyal)   _____
4. (royal)   roial   _____
5. (annoy)   annoi   _____
6. toi   (toy)   _____

Multiplying Two- and Three-Digit Numbers

Rule:
1. Multiply ones by ones, tens, and hundreds. Regroup as needed.
2. Multiply tens by ones, tens, and hundreds. Regroup as needed.
3. Add the two numbers to find the final product.

Example:

```
 325      325      325
x 43     x 43     x 43
 975      975      975
        13000   +13000
                 13,975
```

Solve the problems.

A. 203 × 12 = 2,436
B. 330 × 25 = 8,250
C. 633 × 61 = 38,613
D. 567 × 38 = 21,546

84

Multiplication Rounding and Estimating

Rule:
Since it is easier to multiply by numbers ending in 0, it can be useful to estimate an approximate answer by rounding.

Example:
26 × 9 =
26 rounds up to 30,
so the estimated product is:
30 × 9 = 270

Round the two-digit factor to the nearest ten. Multiply to find the estimated product.

A. 18 → 20 × 2 = 40
B. 23 → 20 × 5 = 100
C. 15 → 20 × 3 = 60
D. 24 → 20 × 9 = 180
E. 58 → 60 × 5 = 300
F. 64 → 60 × 7 = 420
G. 75 → 80 × 4 = 320
H. 81 → 80 × 8 = 640

Adjectives

Use the line in front of each noun to write an adjective that describes the noun.

1. __Answers will vary.__ rain
2. _____ table
3. _____ flower
4. _____ day
5. _____ fruit
6. _____ petal
7. _____ grass
8. _____ friend
9. _____ lake
10. _____ house

85

Prefixes and Suffixes

Base Words are the root words that are used to make other words.
helpful
The root word is help.

Prefixes are letters that are put in front of base words to change the meaning of the base words.
rewrite
The prefix re changes the meaning of the base word write.

Suffixes are letters added to the end of base words to change the meaning of the base word.
healthy
The suffix y changes the meaning of the base word health.

For each question below, decide which part of the word is highlighted in blue. Write base word, prefix, or suffix on the line.

1. punish**ment** base word
2. dark**ness** suffix
3. **dis**appear prefix
4. **pre**cook prefix
5. **pre**soak base word
6. proud**ly** suffix
7. place**ment** suffix
8. **dis**trust prefix
9. color**less** suffix
10. friend**ly** base word
11. sick**ness** base word
12. sugar**less** base word
13. fool**ish** suffix
14. brown**ish** suffix
15. **re**fill prefix
16. **re**pay base word
17. **un**sure prefix
18. lone**ly** suffix

86

Capitalization

In the story below, circle each letter that should be a capital letter. Add an ending to the story.

my birthday

today is my birthday. i am nine years old. i was born on wednesday, april 12, in billings, montana. my family will celebrate my birthday tonight. mom will cook her special spaghetti dinner just for me. dad will be home from work early. my brother, david, and my sister, rose, will be here, too. after dinner grandma and grandpa will come. we will all eat cake and ice cream. they will sing "happy birthday" to me. then . . .

Endings will vary.

_____

87

Fact and Opinion

A **fact** is something that is real and could happen.
There are apples on the tree.

An **opinion** is something that is believed to be true but may not be.
Those apples are beautiful.

Mark each sentence with an **F** for fact and an **O** for opinion.

F 1. My mother fixes dinner every night at 6:00.
O 2. Chocolate pie is the best dessert.
F 3. The state of Wisconsin is a part of the United States.
F 4. People can go to a movie theater to watch movies.
O 5. It is more fun to rent a movie and watch it at home than to go to a theater.

Problem Solving with Multiplication

Solve the word problems. Show your work and write the answers in the space provided.

A. Sophia's Bakery sold 8 cakes each day for 21 days. How many cakes did the bakery sell in all?
   168 cakes

B. Regina made 49 gift baskets each week for 5 weeks. Estimate how many gift baskets she made.
   250 gift baskets

C. For 21 days of camp, Melanie collected 2 souvenirs each day. How many souvenirs did she collect in all?
   42 souvenirs

D. Donna sold 136 bags of popcorn at the movie theater for 24 days. Estimate to find out about how many bags of popcorn Donna sold.
   140 × 20 = 2,800 bags of popcorn

88

Classification

The words below all have something in common. What heading can you give the list that will name all the words? Write a heading on the line Main Heading. Sort the words in the box into two categories. Write the words on the lines. Write a subheading for each group.

big	bitty	enormous	fat	giant	gigantic
great	huge	large	little	long	mammoth
miniature	petite	short	skinny	slight	small
tall	teeny	thin	tiny	vast	wee

Size
Main Heading

| **Big** | **Small** |
Subheading	Subheading
big	bitty
enormous	little
fat	miniature
giant	petite
gigantic	short
great	skinny
huge	slight
large	small
long	teeny
mammoth	thin
tall	tiny
vast	wee

89

Telling Time

Read each problem and circle the correct answer for each.

A. Which clock shows 8:30?

B. Which clock has the same time as the first one?
   4:15

C. Which clock shows 15 minutes before 7?
   6:45

D. Quarter past four is another way of saying which of the following times?
   4:15

Beginning Digraphs: ch, sh, th

Say the name of each picture. Circle the beginning digraph.

1. th
2. sh
3. sh
4. ch

Say the name of each picture. Write the beginning digraph ch, sh, or th to complete the word.

5. ch urch
6. ch icken
7. sh ell
8. th imble

90

Beginning Digraph ph

Read the words. Underline the beginning digraph ph in each word.

1. physical
2. pharmacy
3. photograph
4. pharaoh
5. phantom
6. phonograph
7. physician
8. photosynthesis
9. phonics

Read the words. Circle each word that begins with the digraph ph. Place an x on any word that does not begin with this digraph.

10. phony
11. (photography)
12. pitch ✗
13. poetry ✗
14. page ✗
15. (phobia)
16. puddle ✗
17. (pharmacist)
18. (phase)
19. please ✗
20. piano ✗
21. paper ✗

Elapsed Time

Find each time. All times are A.M. Write the answer on the line provided.

A. 30 minutes after → 10:30 A.M.
B. 15 minutes after → 11:45 A.M.
C. 15 minutes after → 5:00 A.M.
D. 30 minutes after → 3:15 A.M.
E. 30 minutes before → 8:15 A.M.
F. 1 hour before → 9:00 A.M.

91

153

Answer Key

Reading a Calendar

Mrs. Simms has two children, Jay and Joy. The calendar shows Jay's baseball games and Joy's soccer games in April. Use the calendar to answer the questions.

April

Sunday	Monday	Tuesday	Wednesday	Thursday	Friday	Saturday
		1 Jay's game	2	3 Jay's game	4	5 Jay's & Joy's games
6	7 Jay's game	8 Jay's game	9	10 Jay's game	11	12
13 Joy's game	14 Jay's game	15 Jay's game	16	17 Jay's game	18	19 Jay's & Joy's games
20	21	22 Jay's game	23	24 Jay's game	25	26 Joy's game
27	28	29 Jay's game	30			

1. Who plays the first game of the month? **Jay**

2. What day of the week is the first game? **Tuesday**

3. Who has more games, Jay or Joy? **Both players have 9 games.**

4. Who has a game on the second Tuesday of the month? **Joy**

5. On April 24, Joy has a game. What day of the week is that? **Thursday**

6. How many games does Joy play on Tuesdays and Saturdays? **4**

7. On which dates do both Jay and Joy have games? **April 5 and 19**

8. A week begins on Sunday and ends on Saturday. In which week are the most games played? **The week of April 13**

9. Are there any days of the week in which no games are played? **yes, Wednesday**

92

Division Facts 0–1

Rules: 0 divide by any number will always equal 0.

Any number divided by 1 will always equal that number.

Examples: $0 \div 5 = 0$ $8 \div 1 = 8$

A. $0 \div 12 = 0$ B. $0 \div 10 = 0$ C. $3 \div 1 = 3$

D. $5 \div 1 = 5$ E. $0 \div 3 = 0$ F. $0 \div 6 = 0$

G. $4 \div 1 = 4$ H. $0 \div 9 = 0$ I. $0 \div 1 = 0$

J. $11 \div 1 = 11$ K. $7 \div 1 = 7$ L. $0 \div 2 = 0$

M. $9 \div 1 = 9$ N. $1 \div 1 = 1$ O. $0 \div 8 = 0$

Beginning Digraph qu

Say the name of each picture. Circle the picture if the word begins with the digraph qu. Put an ✗ on the picture if the word does not begin with qu.

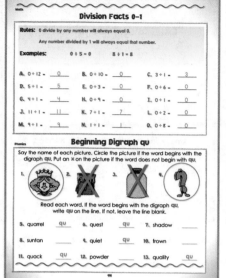

Read each word. If the word begins with the digraph qu, write qu on the line. If not, leave the line blank.

5. quarrel **qu**   6. quest **qu**   7. shadow ___

8. suntan ___   9. quiet **qu**   10. frown ___

11. quack **qu**   12. powder ___   13. quality **qu**

94

Prefixes and Suffixes

Divide the words below by separating the prefixes, suffixes, and base words. **Note:** Sometimes the silent e is removed from the base word when a suffix is added. Example: remove – removable. Add the silent e to the base words that need it.

		Prefix	Base Word	Suffix
1.	refreshment	re	fresh	ment
2.	undependable	un	depend	able
3.	enlargement	en	large	ment
4.	unbelievable	un	believe	able
5.	disappointment	dis	appoint	ment
6.	untruthful	un	truth	ful
7.	prearrangement	pre	arrange	ment

Division Facts 2–4

Rule: 10 items placed in groups of two equal 5 groups.

Example: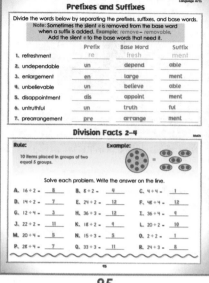

Solve each problem. Write the answer on the line.

A. $16 \div 2 = 8$ B. $8 \div 2 = 4$ C. $4 \div 4 = 1$

D. $14 \div 2 = 7$ E. $24 \div 2 = 12$ F. $48 \div 4 = 12$

G. $12 \div 4 = 3$ H. $36 \div 3 = 12$ I. $36 \div 4 = 9$

J. $22 \div 2 = 11$ K. $18 \div 2 = 9$ L. $20 \div 2 = 10$

M. $20 \div 4 = 5$ N. $15 \div 3 = 5$ O. $2 \div 2 = 1$

P. $28 \div 4 = 7$ Q. $33 \div 3 = 11$ R. $24 \div 2 = 12$

95

Division Facts 1–5

Divide to solve the problems in the problem list. Then, find the same problems in the puzzle. Circle each hidden problem and write ÷ and = in the correct places. Problems are hidden across and down.

Problem List

$6 \div 2 = 3$
$4 \div 2 = 2$
$3 \div 3 = 1$
$15 \div 5 = 3$
$20 \div 5 = 4$
$25 \div 5 = 5$
$10 \div 5 = 2$
$8 \div 4 = 2$
$4 \div 3 = 3$
$20 \div 4 = 5$
$15 \div 3 = 5$
$12 \div 3 = 4$
$12 \div 4 = 3$
$5 \div 5 = 1$
$10 \div 5 = 2$
$8 \div 2 = 4$
$16 \div 4 = 4$

96

Division Facts 5–7

Solve each problem. Then, write the answer on the line provided.

A. $30 \div 5 = 6$ $54 \div 6 = 9$ $49 \div 7 = 7$

B. $12 \div 6 = 2$ $15 \div 5 = 3$ $60 \div 6 = 10$

C. $40 \div 5 = 8$ $28 \div 7 = 4$ $25 \div 5 = 5$

D. $18 \div 6 = 2$ $70 \div 7 = 10$ $60 \div 5 = 12$

E. $42 \div 6 = 7$ $63 \div 7 = 9$ $77 \div 7 = 11$

F. $35 \div 7 = 5$ $7 \div 7 = 1$ $14 \div 7 = 2$

G. $48 \div 6 = 8$ $36 \div 6 = 6$ $10 \div 5 = 2$

H. $20 \div 5 = 4$ $55 \div 5 = 11$ $84 \div 7 = 12$

I. $56 \div 7 = 8$ $45 \div 5 = 9$ $66 \div 6 = 11$

97

Ending Blend -mp

Add the ending blend mp to each set of letters. Say the words.

1. bu **mp**   2. ca **mp**   3. stu **mp**   4. lu **mp**

5. swa **mp**   6. shri **mp**   7. pu **mp**   8. cla **mp**

Look at each picture. Circle the mp word that names each picture and write the word on the line.

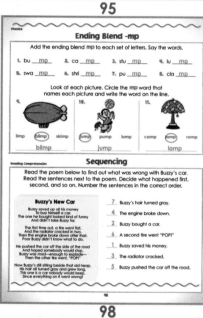

9. limp (blimp) skimp → **blimp**

10. (jump) pump lump → **jump**

11. camp (lamp) ramp → **lamp**

Sequencing

Read the poem below to find out what was wrong with Buzzy's car. Read the sentences next to the poem. Decide what happened first, second, and so on. Number the sentences in the correct order.

Buzzy's New Car

Buzzy saved up all his money
To buy himself a car.
The one he bought looked kind of funny
And didn't take Buzzy far.

The first time out, a tire went flat.
And the radiator cracked in two.
Then the engine broke down after that.
Poor Buzzy didn't know what to do.

He pushed the car off the side of the road
And hoped somebody would stop.
Buzzy was mad—enough to explode—
Then the other tire went, "POP!"

Now Buzzy's still sitting beside that old heap.
His hair all turned gray and gray along.
This one is a car nobody would keep.
Since everything on it went wrong!

7 Buzzy's hair turned gray.
4 The engine broke down.
2 Buzzy bought a car.
6 A second tire went "POP!"
1 Buzzy saved his money.
3 The radiator cracked.
5 Buzzy pushed the car off the road.

98

Division Facts 8–9

Solve each problem. Write the answer on the line provided.

A. $16 \div 8 = 2$ $24 \div 8 = 3$ $54 \div 9 = 6$

B. $36 \div 9 = 4$ $72 \div 9 = 8$ $56 \div 8 = 7$

C. $88 \div 8 = 11$ $32 \div 8 = 4$ $72 \div 8 = 9$

D. $45 \div 9 = 5$ $81 \div 9 = 9$ $80 \div 8 = 10$

E. $27 \div 9 = 3$ $90 \div 9 = 10$ $96 \div 8 = 12$

F. $40 \div 8 = 5$ $64 \div 8 = 6$ $63 \div 9 = 7$

G. $8 \div 8 = 1$ $18 \div 9 = 2$ $108 \div 9 = 12$

H. $48 \div 8 = 6$ $9 \div 9 = 1$ $99 \div 9 = 11$

99

Division Facts 1–9

Divide to solve the problems and then color.

9 = red   7 = orange
5 = purple   8 = continue
black

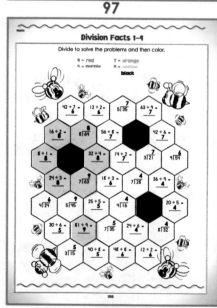

100

Beat the Clock (Division Facts 1–9)

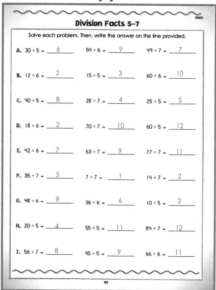

Time: _____   **Number correct:** _____

103

Answer Key

Page 104

Ending Blend -nd

Look at the pictures and say the words.
Circle the nd word that names each picture.

1. (sand) fond wand
2. land stand (round)
3. bond (band) bend

Read each sentence. Circle the nd word that completes the sentence.

4. We left at the _____ of the movie. land (end) suspend
5. Be careful when you _____ on the stool. remind (stand) hand
6. I saw a penny on the _____. wind send (ground)
7. Guide dogs help the _____. (blind) spend fund

Decimal Place Value

Rule:	Example:
The decimal point separates the ones digit from the tenths digit.	23.45 = 2 3 . 4 5 tens ones tenths hundredths

Underline the digit in the tenths place.

A. 35.15 B. 11.18 C. 65.56 D. 50.63
E. 10.93 F. 9.95 G. 19.81 H. 19.58

Underline the digit in the hundredths place.

I. 19.62 J. 6.78 K. 73.17 L. 35.18
M. 25.84 N. 22.15 O. 99.99 P. 18.33

104

Page 105

Proofreading

Add punctuation marks and capital letters where they are needed in the story below. Add an ending to the story.

The mother bird was busy with her three new babies. They were growing so quickly. Soon they would begin flying. They were always hungry. She could never seem to find enough food to keep them full. Back and forth she flew all day long with worms and bugs.

Chirpy was the smallest of the three babies. He was also the bravest. He liked to jump to the edge of the nest to see his new world. The mother bird warned him to be careful. She said that he might fall from the nest. There were cats in the yard below. How would he get home if he fell out of the nest?

The mother bird flew away to get the babies' dinner. Chirpy hopped right up on the edge of the nest. Suddenly his foot slipped. He began to fall and . . .

_____

_____

Stories will vary.

_____

_____

105

Page 107

Vocabulary Assessment

Read the first part of each sentence. Choose the word that means about the same thing as the highlighted word or phrase. Fill in the circle next to the correct answer.

1. To wash or clean by rubbing hard is to . . .
   ○ dimple
   ○ crumble
   ● scrub

2. A group of related sentences is a . . .
   ● paragraph
   ○ sniffle
   ○ mission

3. When you get something, you . . .
   ○ reappear
   ○ navigate
   ● receive

4. The smallest amount is the . . .
   ○ fate
   ○ mutter
   ● least

5. Two things that are completely different are called . . .
   ○ onward
   ● opposite
   ○ mischief

6. To be thankful is to be . . .
   ○ necessary
   ○ sloppy
   ● grateful

7. Anything that happened before now is in the . . .
   ○ future
   ● past
   ○ native

8. A book that lists meanings of words is a . . .
   ○ marvel
   ○ represent
   ● dictionary

9. When you stay behind, you . . .
   ● remain
   ○ hitch
   ○ express

10. To make a person do something he doesn't want to do is to . . .
    ● force
    ○ outwit
    ○ link

107

Page 108

Compound Words

Finish the story below using the words in the word bank. Write the compound words in the blanks where they belong.

backyard   fireflies   lonesome   moonlight   waterproof
campfire   flashlight   midnight   rattlesnake   weekend

Camping

Last **weekend** I went camping. I had a **waterproof** tent in case it rained. It was great fun at first. The **fireflies** were glowing in the bushes. I built a warm **campfire**. The **moonlight** was so bright I didn't even need my **flashlight**. About **midnight**, I became **lonesome** and a little scared. I thought I heard a **rattlesnake** near my tent. Thank goodness I was in my own **backyard**.

Parts of Speech

Read each sentence. List each word on the line beside the correct part of speech.

1. These berries smash easily.
   noun **berries**   adjective **These**
   verb **smash**   adverb **easily**

2. Ten soldiers march together.
   noun **soldiers**   adjective **Ten**
   verb **march**   adverb **together**

3. The big pillow belongs here.
   noun **pillow**   adjective **big**
   verb **belongs**   adverb **here**

108

Page 109

Reading and Writing Decimals

Decimals are numbers used to represent fractions. They contain a decimal point. Change the numbers below from word form to decimals.

Example: six and five-tenths is written 6.5

A. two-tenths   .2
B. five-tenths   .5
C. seven-hundredths   .07
D. one and nine-hundredths   1.09
E. four and six-tenths   4.6
F. fifteen and eight-hundredths   15.08

Ending Blends: -lk, -nk, -sk

Say the name of each picture. Circle the word that names the picture and underline the ending.

1. (trunk) silk task
2. yolk (desk) sank
3. walk (bank) ask

Circle the ending blend in each word.

4. ki(sk)   5. ta(lk)   6. hu(sk)   7. thi(nk)
8. fri(sk)   9. wi(nk)   10. su(lk)   11. bli(nk)
12. ta(lk)   13. ya(nk)   14. bri(sk)   15. sku(lk)

109

Page 110

Cause and Effect

A cause is the reason something happens.
An effect is what happens.

Example:
The cat scratched me because I pulled its tail.
Cause— I pulled its tail.
Effect— The cat scratched me.

Underline the cause in each sentence.

1. The rain started, and the boys ran for shelter.
2. Mother served ice cream and cake after dinner because it is my favorite dessert.
3. Since I cannot swim, my dad will not let me go to the lake by myself.
4. Joshua sleeps most of the day because he is a baby.
5. Mary cannot go to school because she is sick.

Circle the effect in each sentence.

6. Noel went to the movies this afternoon because he was bored.
7. I was so tired that I went to bed early last night.
8. Since she had work to do, Anna did not watch television today.
9. I made an A on my test because I studied.
10. I skinned my knee when I fell off my bike.

110

Page 111

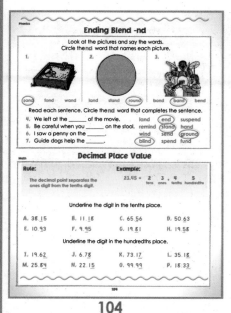

Crossword Puzzles

Remove pages 111–114. Cut along dashed lines. Staple pages in order.

Use the word list to solve the crossword puzzle.

Word List
dragon   moat   queen
knight   armor   jester
king   castle   farmers

Across
were people who grew food for the king.
amused the king by clowning and joking.
was a large stone home for a king.
was a legendary fire-breathing creature.

Down
1. The wife of the king was called the
2. A man who fought for the king was called a
3. The ruler of the land was called the
4. The water-filled area that surrounded the castle was called the
5. The metal suit worn by a knight was called

111

Page 112

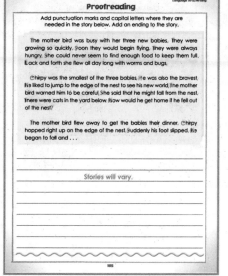

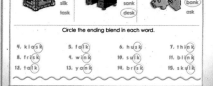

Use the word list to solve the crossword puzzle.

Word List
grow   forest
hibernate   cave
fur   paw

Across
4. Bears have sharp
6. Bears sleep, or ____, all winter.
8. A large brownish bear found in North America is a

Down
1. A bear might make its home in a
2. Body bears are covered with
3. A toy bear with stuffing inside is called a

Use the word list to solve the crossword puzzle.

Word List
dessert   fork
utensil   meals
beverage   restaurant
napkin   spoon

The ____ words in the kitchen preparing meals.
A place to go out to eat is a
Chocolate cake is my favorite
I like ranch dressing on my
Knives, forks, and spoons are called
Another word for drink is
Wipe your mouth with a
takes orders in a restaurant.

112

Page 113

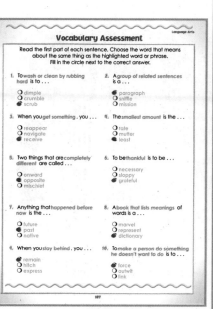

Use the word list to solve the crossword puzzle.

Word List
pool   giggles
water   bubbles
raft   ocean
sunshine   blow
dive   stroke
splash

Across
5. Swimmers use their legs to ____ in the water.
A person wears ____ over his eyes to help him see underwater.
Air ____ float to the surface of the water.
A ____ can be used to ride on the waves.
The large body of water at the beach is called the

Down
1. You ____ into the water when you jump head first.
A large container with water for swimming is called a
Don't dive into the pool if you don't know the
A swimmer's arm motion is called a
Jumping into water causes a

Use the word list to solve the crossword puzzle.

Word List
hail   clouds
rain   sunshine
fog   snow
storm   wind
thunder   blizzard

Across
The ____ feels warm.
Wind along with rain, thunder and lightning is usually called a
It's snowing so hard I can't see. This is called a
Water falling from the sky is
March is a month with strong

Down
1. Boom! It must be
2. A funnel of wind is called a
3. Before a storm, you often see many
4. A cloud near the ground that is hard to see through is
7. Rain in the form of small, frozen pellets is called

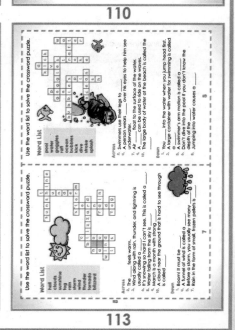

113

Answer Key

Page 114

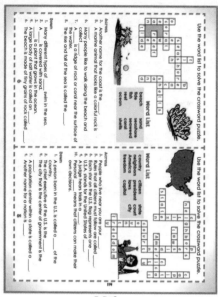

Use the word list to solve the crossword puzzle.

Across
1. Another name for the coast is the ___.
3. A marine animal that looks like a colorful rock is ___.
5. Many people like to walk along the beach to collect ___.
7. ___ is a ridge of rock or coral near the beach that birds like to walk on.
8. A large body of salt water is called an ___.

Down
2. The rise and fall of the sea is called the ___.
4. A person can ___ swim in the sea.
6. ___ is covered with sand.
9. The ___ is a pointed growth in the ocean.
10. A large body of salt water is called the ___.
11. The beach is made of tiny grains of rock called ___.

Word List
beach, tide, fish, ocean, sand, shells, seaweed, coral, walk

Use the word list to solve the crossword puzzle.

Across
1. People who live near you are your ___.
3. Rules that all citizens must follow are called ___.
5. Each star on the U.S. flag represents one ___.
6. U.S.A. stands for the United States of ___.
7. A judge hears trials in a ___.
8. A population center within a state is called a ___.
9. Another name for a nation is ___.

Down
2. A person born in the U.S. is called a ___.
4. The chief executive of the U.S. is the ___.
10. The city that is the center of government is the ___.
11. Personal freedoms means that citizens can make their own decisions.

Word List
country, neighbors, state, America, freedom, laws, capital, court, city

Page 116

Ending Blends: -ft, -nt, -st

Say the name of each picture.
Write the ending blends, ft, nt, or st, to complete the word.

1. li st
2. fore st
3. te nt
4. pla nt
5. a nt
6. wri st
7. gi ft
8. ne st

Adding and Subtracting Decimals

Rule:
1. Line up the decimal points.
2. Start from the far right.
3. Regroup as needed.
4. Bring the decimal point down to the answer.

Example:
$3.76 + 1.59 =$
$3.76 + 1.59 = 5.35$

A. 6.5 + 7.3 = 13.8	B. 2.7 + 4.1 = 6.8	C. 6.5 − 1.2 = 5.3	D. 5.9 − 2.5 = 3.4
E. 12.5 + 9.4 = 21.9	F. 0.42 + 0.36 = .78	G. 2.41 + 7.49 = 9.90	H. 8.7 + 5.5 = 14.2
I. 3.8 + 4.9 = 8.7	J. 10.5 − 7.7 = 2.8	K. 4.13 − 2.95 = 1.18	L. 0.28 + .87 = 1.15

Page 117

Persuasive Paragraphs

You must convince your mom to let you play in the rain.
Give your reasons. Then, ask again.

Title	
Question	May I
Reasons	1.
	2. Details will vary.
	3.
	4.
Ask again	

Use the sentences above to write a paragraph. Ask the question, state the reasons, and then ask the question again. Indent the first sentence. Use capital letters and periods. Remember to give your paragraph a title.

Paragraphs will vary.

Page 118

Syllables

Find out how many syllables are in each word by counting the number of vowels you hear when you say the word. Write the number on the blank.

1. machine — 2
2. somersault — 3
3. peanut — 2
4. neighborhood — 3
5. astronaut — 3
6. koala — 3
7. dragon — 2
8. itch — 1
9. hero — 2
10. auditorium — 5
11. longitude — 3
12. congratulate — 4
13. frog — 1
14. multiplication — 5
15. Canada — 3
16. zipper — 2
17. gulf — 1
18. lasagna — 3

Adding and Subtracting Fractions

Rule:
When adding or subtracting fractions with the same denominator:
1. Add or subtract their numerators.
2. Write that number over the same denominator.

Examples:
$$\frac{3}{8} + \frac{2}{8} = \frac{5}{8}$$
$$\frac{9}{10} - \frac{3}{10} = \frac{6}{10}$$

Solve each problem. Write the answer in the space provided.

A. $\frac{4}{7} - \frac{2}{7} = \frac{2}{7}$
B. $\frac{1}{3} + \frac{1}{3} = \frac{2}{3}$
C. $\frac{7}{8} - \frac{5}{8} = \frac{3}{8}$
D. $\frac{3}{11} + \frac{5}{11} = \frac{8}{11}$
E. $\frac{10}{25} - \frac{3}{25} = \frac{7}{25}$
F. $\frac{1}{5} - \frac{1}{5} = 0$

Page 119

Writing Stories

Write a story about the picture. Be sure to use capital letters and periods where needed. Give your story a title.

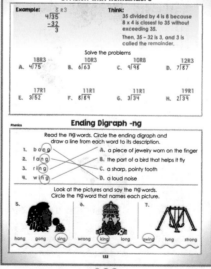

Things to Think About
Who is this story about?
Where does this story take place?
How does the story begin?
What happens next?
How will the story end?

Stories will vary.

Page 120

Division

Example:
$6\overline{)30}$ = 5
-30
0

Think: 6 divides evenly into 30, leaving no remainder.

Solve the problems.

A. $5\overline{)35} = 7$
B. $7\overline{)14} = 2$
C. $4\overline{)28} = 7$
D. $3\overline{)24} = 8$
E. $3\overline{)18} = 6$
F. $8\overline{)56} = 7$
G. $3\overline{)33} = 11$
H. $8\overline{)64} = 8$

Synonyms

Synonyms are words that have the same or almost the same meaning.
Examples: work – toil, small – little

Circle the two words in each row that are synonyms.

1. (beautiful) clever (pretty) eager
2. (wicked) (evil) curious calm
3. hymn (honor) fall (respect)
4. sing volley (clap) (applaud)
5. (get) return area (receive)
6. (unhappy) tender shock (sad)
7. end (plead) (beg) cause

Page 121

Ending Digraphs: -ch, -sh, -th

Say the name of each picture.
Circle the word that names the picture and write the word.

1. much, which, (couch) — couch
2. (brush), wish, dish — brush
3. broth, with, (mouth) — mouth
4. wreath, teach, (bath) — bath
5. sloth, (peach), beach — peach
6. rush, (bush), ash — bush

Division with No Remainders

Example:
$4\overline{)48} = 12$
-4
08
-8
0

Think: 4 divides evenly into 48, leaving no remainder.

Solve the problems.

A. $2\overline{)64} = 32$
B. $9\overline{)90} = 10$
C. $6\overline{)72} = 12$
D. $4\overline{)100} = 25$
E. $3\overline{)69} = 13$
F. $3\overline{)36} = 12$
G. $6\overline{)84} = 14$
H. $5\overline{)125} = 25$

Page 122

Division with Remainders

Example:
$4\overline{)35} = 8\ R3$
-32
3

Think: 35 divided by 4 is 8 because 8 x 4 is closest to 35 without exceeding 35. Then, 35 − 32 is 3, and 3 is called the remainder.

Solve the problems.

A. $4\overline{)75} = 18R3$
B. $6\overline{)63} = 10R3$
C. $9\overline{)98} = 10R8$
D. $7\overline{)87} = 12R3$
E. $3\overline{)52} = 17R1$
F. $8\overline{)89} = 11R1$
G. $3\overline{)34} = 11R1$
H. $2\overline{)39} = 19R1$

Ending Digraph -ng

Read the ng words. Circle the ending digraph and draw a line from each word to its description.

1. ba n g — D. a loud noise
2. fa n g — C. a sharp, pointy tooth
3. ri n g — A. a piece of jewelry worn on the finger
4. wi n g — B. the part of a bird that helps it fly

Look at the pictures and say the ng words.
Circle the ng word that names each picture.

5. hang gong (sing)
6. wrong (king) long
7. (swing) lung strong

Page 123

Ending Digraph -dge

Read the words. Circle each word that ends with the digraph dge.

1. (sludge)
2. clay
3. (partridge)
4. insect
5. (ridge)
6. wade
7. (fudge)
8. age
9. (lodge)
10. (hedge)
11. sled
12. ride

Look at the pictures and say the words. Fill in the circle next to the dge word that names each picture.

13. ● badge / ○ edge
14. ● judge / ○ fudge
15. ○ lodge / ● bridge

Problem Solving with Division

Solve the problems. Show your work.

A. Stan had 32 bags of popcorn to sell at the snack bar. He sold all of the popcorn to 8 customers. If each customer bought the same number of popcorn bags, how many bags did each buy? — **4 popcorn bags**

B. Ms. Davis drove 325 miles in 5 days. If she drove the same number of miles each day, how many miles did she drive? — **65 miles**

C. Phil sold 146 magazine subscriptions. He worked for 2 weeks and sold the same amount each week. How many subscriptions did he sell each week? — **73 subscriptions**

D. Reginald has 162 seeds to plant in his garden. If he digs 18 holes in the soil and wants to distribute the seeds equally, how many seeds can he put in each hole? — **9 seeds**

Answer Key

Problem Solving with Decimals

A. Complete the next 3 decimals in each sequence.

.15, .25, .35, .45, __55__ __65__ __75__

3.8, 3.7, 3.6, 3.5, __3.4__ __3.3__ __3.2__

B. Using the greater than (>) and less than (<) symbols, write two number sentences using the following numbers: 3.4, 3.5

3.4 < 3.5
3.5 < 3.4

C. Place the following numbers in order from least to greatest.

2.5, 5.2, 4.2, 4.12, 5.25

__2.5__, __4.12__, __4.2__, __5.2__, __5.25__

D. Chuck's weekly allowance is $5.00. After buying a package of beef jerky for $1.67, how much money does he have left?

$5.00
−1.67
$3.33

Antonyms

Antonyms are words that have opposite meanings.
Examples: hot – cold, near – far

Circle the two words in each row that are antonyms.

1. juggle ⟨approve⟩ explode ⟨dislike⟩
2. grasp fact ⟨achieve⟩ ⟨fail⟩
3. sure blot ⟨calm⟩ ⟨stormy⟩
4. ⟨even⟩ escape plain ⟨uneven⟩
5. ⟨wrong⟩ call wait ⟨right⟩
6. ⟨shame⟩ ⟨honor⟩ helpful below

Sequencing

Sequencing means to put things in the proper order.

The hot chocolate recipe in the box is all mixed up.
After reading all the steps, put the recipe in the correct order.
Some steps have already been written.

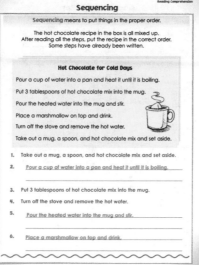

Hot Chocolate for Cold Days

Pour a cup of water into a pan and heat it until it is boiling.

Put 3 tablespoons of hot chocolate mix into the mug.

Pour the heated water into the mug and stir.

Place a marshmallow on top and drink.

Turn off the stove and remove the hot water.

Take out a mug, a spoon, and hot chocolate mix and set aside.

1. Take out a mug, a spoon, and hot chocolate mix and set aside.
2. _Pour a cup of water into a pan and heat it until it is boiling._
3. Put 3 tablespoons of hot chocolate mix into the mug.
4. Turn off the stove and remove the hot water.
5. _Pour the heated water into the mug and stir._
6. _Place a marshmallow on top and drink._

Graphic Art Project

Follow the directions below to make a colorful drawing.

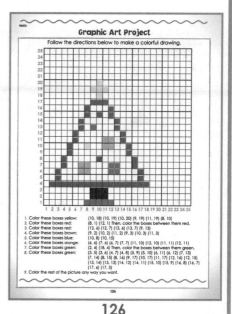

1. Color these boxes yellow: (10, 18) (10, 19) (10, 20) (9, 19) (11, 19) (8, 10)
2. Color these boxes red: (8, 1) (12, 1) Then, color the boxes between them red.
3. Color these boxes blue: (12, 6) (12, 7) (13, 6) (13, 7) (9, 13)
4. Color these boxes brown: (9, 2) (10, 2) (11, 2) (9, 3) (10, 3) (11, 3)
5. Color these boxes blue: (10, 8) (10, 15)
6. Color these boxes orange: (6, 7) (6, 7) (7, 7) (11, 10) (12, 10) (11, 11) (12, 7)
7. Color these boxes green: (2, 4) (18, 4) Then, color the boxes between them green.
8. Color these boxes green: (3, 5) (3, 6) (4, 7) (4, 8) (5, 9) (5, 10) (6, 11) (6, 12) (7, 13) (7, 14) (8, 15) (8, 16) (9, 17) (10, 17) (11, 17) (12, 16) (12, 15) (13, 14) (13, 13) (14, 12) (14, 11) (15, 10) (15, 9) (16, 8) (16, 7) (17, 6) (17, 5)
9. Color the rest of the picture any way you want.

Silent Letter in "tch"

Read the words. If the word ends with the digraph tch, fill in the circle and circle the ending digraph.

1. ● pi⟨tch⟩
2. ○ search
3. ● hu⟨tch⟩
4. ○ fight
5. ○ with
6. ● su⟨tch⟩
7. ○ wrath
8. ● twi⟨tch⟩
9. ● pa⟨tch⟩
10. ● ha⟨tch⟩
11. ● fe⟨tch⟩
12. ● clu⟨tch⟩

Say the name of each picture. Circle the word that names the picture.

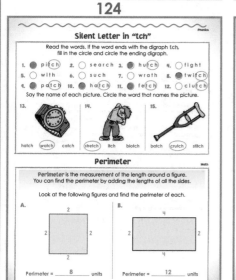

13. hatch ⟨watch⟩ catch
14. ⟨stretch⟩ itch blotch
15. batch ⟨crutch⟩ stitch

Perimeter

Perimeter is the measurement of the length around a figure. You can find the perimeter by adding the lengths of all the sides.

Look at the following figures and find the perimeter of each.

A. (square, sides 2, 2, 2, 2)

Perimeter = __8__ units

B. (rectangle, sides 4, 2, 4, 2)

Perimeter = __12__ units

Subject-Verb Agreement

Complete each sentence with the correct verb form.

1. In the summer, I __work__ as a detective. (work / works)
2. I __solve__ neighborhood mysteries. (solve / solves)
3. When Mrs. Carter __loses__ her cat, I help her find it. (lose / loses)
4. If there are footprints, I __find__ out whose they are. (find / finds)
5. My friend Jim __writes__ me secret messages. (write / writes)
6. I __use__ my decoder to figure them out. (use / uses)
7. I __keep__ my detective kit in a secret place. (keep / keeps)
8. Only Mom and Dad __know__ where it is. (know / knows)

Predicting

Read the paragraph. Then answer the questions.

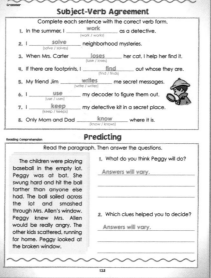

The children were playing baseball in the empty lot. Peggy was at bat. She swung hard and hit the ball farther than anyone else had. The ball sailed across the lot and smashed through Mrs. Allen's window. Peggy knew Mrs. Allen would be really angry. The other kids scattered, running for home. Peggy looked at the broken window.

1. What do you think Peggy will do?
   Answers will vary.

2. Which clues helped you to decide?
   Answers will vary.

Metric Length

Rules:
1 centimeter (cm) = 10 millimeters (mm)
1 decimeter (dm) = 10 centimeters (cm)
1 meter (m) = 100 centimeters (cm)
1 kilometer (km) = 1,000 meters

Example:
Is 1 m longer than 120 cm?
1 m = 100 cm, so 1 meter is not longer than 120 cm.
Answer: No

Answer each question. Write yes or no on the line provided.

A. Is 15 cm longer than 1 dm? __yes__
B. Is 5 dm longer than 1 m? __no__
C. Is 900 m longer than 1 km? __no__
D. Is 1 m longer than 90 cm? __yes__
E. Is 1 m longer than 1 dm? __yes__
F. Is 20 cm longer than 1 m? __no__
G. Is 5 mm longer than 1 cm? __no__
H. Is 2 km longer than 1,500 m? __yes__
I. Is 2 cm longer than 10 mm? __yes__
J. Is 15 cm longer than 1 m? __no__

Silent Letter in "kn"

Read each riddle. Write the kn word from the word list that answers the riddle.

| knee | knife | knot | knapsack | knight | knoll | knocker |

1. I can be found on a door. You use me to let someone know you are at the door. What am I? __knocker__
2. You can put things inside of me and carry me. What am I? __knapsack__
3. I helped protect the king. I wore armor. Who am I? __knight__
4. I am part of your body. You can find me on your leg. What am I? __knee__
5. You must be careful with me. I help cut your food. What am I? __knife__
6. I am a small, round hill. What am I? __knoll__
7. You can tie me in a piece of string. What am I? __knot__

Silent Letter in "wr"

Write the letters wr in front of each set of letters. Say the words.

1. __wr__inkle
2. __wr__eath
3. __wr__ong
4. __wr__angle
5. __wr__apper
6. __wr__eck
7. __wr__estle
8. __wr__ap

Say each wr word. Circle the picture of the word.

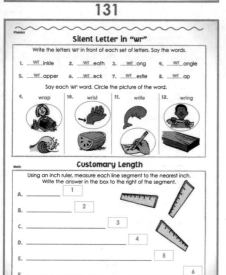

9. wrap
10. wrist
11. write
12. wring

Customary Length

Using an inch ruler, measure each line segment to the nearest inch. Write the answer in the box to the right of the segment.

A. 1
B. 2
C. 3
D. 4
E. 5
F. 6

Customary Capacity

Rules:
2 cups = 1 pint
2 pints = 1 quart
4 quarts = 1 gallon

Example:
Is one cup greater than, less than, or equal to 1 pint?
If 2 cups = 1 pint
then 1 cup is __less than__ 1 pint.

Complete each sentence using more than, less than, or equal to. Write your answer on the line.

A. 2 pints are __equal to__ 1 quart.
B. 1 pint is __less than__ 1 quart.
C. 3 quarts are __less than__ 1 gallon.
D. 3 cups are __less than__ 1 quart.
E. 1 gallon is __more than__ 1 pint.
F. 6 pints are __equal to__ 3 quarts.
G. 2 pints are __equal to__ 4 cups.
H. 8 quarts are __equal to__ 2 gallons.

Silent Letter in "ck"

Read the words. Circle each word that ends with the letters ck.

1. jazz
2. speech
3. mask
4. crutch
5. ⟨rock⟩
6. ⟨stick⟩
7. ⟨click⟩
8. ⟨lock⟩
9. lake
10. ⟨quack⟩
11. ⟨quick⟩
12. ⟨sick⟩

Read each word group. Write the ck word from the word list that belongs with the group.

| Word List | sock | stick | neck | quick | rock | truck |

13. fast, speedy, __quick__
14. log, twig, __stick__
15. shoulder, arm, __neck__
16. stone, pebble, __rock__
17. shoe, feet, __sock__
18. car, motorcycle, __truck__

Silent Letter in "mb"

Say the name of each picture. Fill in the circle next to the mb word that names the picture.

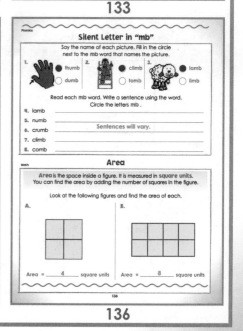

1. ● thumb / ○ dumb
2. ● climb / ○ limb
3. ● lamb / ○ limb

Read each mb word. Write a sentence using the word. Circle the letters mb.

4. lamb
5. numb
6. crumb _____ Sentences will vary.
7. climb
8. comb

Area

Area is the space inside a figure. It is measured in square units. You can find the area by adding the number of squares in the figure.

Look at the following figures and find the area of each.

A.

Area = __4__ square units

B.

Area = __8__ square units

Answer Key

Reading a Map Grid

Sometimes a map is drawn with a grid. The number coordinates on the map grid below are located on both sides of the map. The letter coordinates are located at the top and bottom of the map.

Look at the locations of the different cities. Write the name of each city on the line beside the matching coordinates at the bottom of the page.

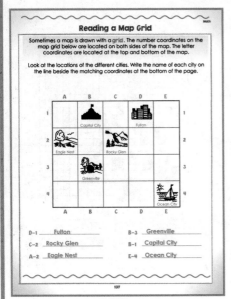

D–1	Fulton	
C–2	Rocky Glen	
A–2	Eagle Nest	
B–3	Greenville	
B–1	Capital City	
E–4	Ocean City	

137

Area and Perimeter

Rules:

Area (A) is the number of square units inside a figure. To find the area of rectangles and squares, multiply the length times the width.

Perimeter (P) is the number of units around a figure. To find the perimeter of rectangles and squares, add the length of all four sides.

Examples:

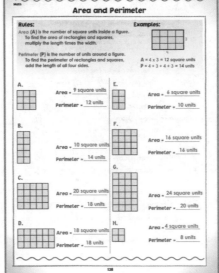

A = 4 × 3 = 12 square units
P = 4 + 3 + 4 + 3 = 14 units

A. Area = 9 square units   Perimeter = 12 units

B. Area = 10 square units   Perimeter = 14 units

C. Area = 20 square units   Perimeter = 18 units

D. Area = 18 square units   Perimeter = 18 units

E. Area = 6 square units   Perimeter = 10 units

F. Area = 16 square units   Perimeter = 16 units

G. Area = 24 square units   Perimeter = 20 units

H. Area = 4 square units   Perimeter = 8 units

138

Outcomes

An outcome is the result of an event.

Decide whether the following outcomes are certain (will definitely happen), possible (might happen), or impossible (will not happen). Write your answer on the line.

1. It will rain tomorrow. ___possible___
2. You will grow to be 50 feet tall. ___impossible___
3. The Vikings will win the Super Bowl next season. ___possible___
4. Tomorrow will be 24 hours long. ___certain___
5. Humans will travel to Mars. ___possible___
6. New Year's Eve will fall on December 31st. ___certain___

Homophones

Homophones are words that sound alike but are spelled differently and have different meanings.
Example: tall – tale

Circle the two words in each row that are homophones.

1. (bear)   seen   saw   (bare)
2. violet   vase   (vain)   (vein)
3. drop   (dew)   down   (due)
4. (tee)   tell   told   (tea)
5. well   (weight)   (wait)   went
6. him   (hair)   (hare)   held

139

Reading a Map

Marcia lives in Flower City. She has a new friend named Tina. Marcia invited Tina to her house for a visit. Marcia drew a map to help Tina find her house.

Look at the map and use it to answer the questions below.

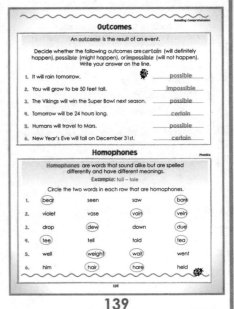

1. The road where Marcia lives is ___Violet Road___.
2. The lane where Tina lives is ___Daisy Lane___.
3. What four roads cross the railroad tracks?
   ___Tulip Avenue, Daisy Lane, Zinnia Street, Daffodil Road___
4. What road intersects both Daffodil Road and Violet Road?
   ___Zinnia Street___
5. How can you get across Bubbling Creek?
   ___Take Tulip Avenue, Crocus Road, or Violet Road___
6. What roads intersect Zinnia Street?
   ___Daffodil Road, Violet Road___

140

Punctuation

Place the correct punctuation mark at the end of each sentence in the story below. Write an ending to the story.

Making Pancakes

My sister and I woke early last Saturday morning. We decided to make breakfast for Mom. We took out the pancake mix. We put the mix in a big bowl. We added eggs and milk. I was stirring the batter. My sister was pouring orange juice. Then, the cat jumped onto the counter. He tipped over the glass of juice and knocked the bowl to the floor. Batter and juice went everywhere! Next . . .

Endings will vary.

141

Understanding What I Read

Read the story. Then answer the questions.

Nightly Navigator

Many people do not realize what bats do for us. They are some of our best nighttime insect exterminators. Over 900 kinds of bats exist in the world today. These bats can be anywhere from one-half inch long to over 15 inches long. Although most bats eat just insects, some dine on fruit and the nectar of flowers. As the only flying mammals on earth, bats should be recognized for their contributions to humans. Aside from controlling the insect population, bats are the main pollinators and seed spreaders for many tropical trees like mangoes, guavas, cashews, cloves, and Brazil nuts. Bats use their sonar-guided mouths and ears to enjoy a nightly dinner of millions of mosquitoes, mayflies, and moths.

1. What is the main idea of this paragraph?
   Most people do not realize what bats do for us.
2. How many different kinds of bats are there in the world?
   Over 900 kinds of bats exist in the world.
3. What do bats like to eat?
   Bats eat insects, fruit, and the nectar of flowers.
4. How large can some species of bats get?
   Bats can grow to over 15 inches long.
5. What kinds of tropical trees depend on the bat for spreading their seeds and for pollination?
   Bats spread seed for mangoes, guavas, cashews, cloves, and Brazil nuts.

142

How to Write a Friendly Letter

Review the five parts of a friendly letter.

July 10, 2002 — date

Dear Tim, — greeting

What a great time we had when you came to visit! I liked playing baseball and football with you. Swimming was fun, too. I hope that you will visit me again soon. — body

Your friend, — closing
Jason — signature

Write a letter to your friend. Talk about the things you like to do together.

(date)
(greeting)
Paragraphs will vary.
(body)
(closing)
(signature)

143

Write a Friendly Letter

Write a letter to a new friend. Be sure to include the five parts of a friendly letter.

Describe yourself.
Tell what you like to do.
Describe your room.
Describe your family.

Paragraphs will vary.

144

Addressing Envelopes

Address the envelopes below using the information given.

The sender is:
Dr. James Madison
38 Carlton Place
Salem, NC 29532

The receiver is:
Ms. Mary Morton
149 Sparrow Street
Tucson, AZ 52974

Dr. James Madison
38 Carlton Place
Salem, NC 29532

Ms. Mary Morton
149 Sparrow Street
Tucson AZ 52974

The sender is:
Mrs. Alice Watson
9 Flag Avenue
Port Huron, MI 48060

The receiver is:
Miss Susan Coats
183 Spring Street
Denver, CO 50738

Mrs. Alice Watson
9 Flag Avenue
Port Huron, MI 48060

Miss Susan Coats
183 Spring Street
Denver, CO 50738

145

Cut-and-Color Awards

Parent: Have your child decorate and color these awards. Fill in your child's name and the date to mark each accomplishment. The awards can be worn as badges or put into small frames.

I can arrange words and titles in alphabetical order!

Name: _____ Date: _____

I can add and subtract LARGE numbers!

Name: _____ Date: _____

I understand base words, prefixes, and suffixes!

Name: _____ Date: _____

I know my multiplication facts!

Name: _____ Date: _____

I know my division facts!

Name: _____ Date: _____

nouns   verbs   adverbs

I know my parts of speech!

adjectives

Name: _____ Date: _____

I can use punctuation correctly!

Name: _____ Date: _____

I know my vowel sounds and consonant blends and digraphs!

Name: _____ Date: _____